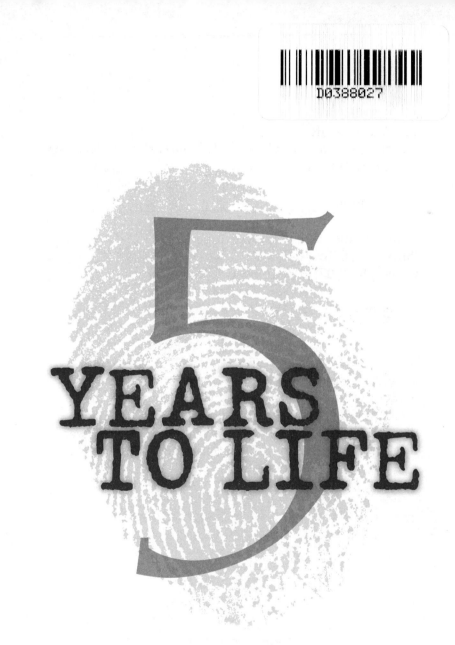

5 YEARS TO LIFE

SAM HUDDLESTON

Five Years to Life
The story of a wayward son and his father's relentless love
By Sam Huddleston

Third edition

Printed in the United States of America
ISBN: 1-880689-16-2
Copyright 2007, 2010, Onward Books, Inc.

Cover design by KeyArt

DEDICATION

This book is dedicated to my wife, Linda, who taught me to dream again.

CONTENTS

Preface 7

Acknowledgements 9

Chapter 1 12

Chapter 2 32

Chapter 3 50

Chapter 4 72

Chapter 5 84

Chapter 6 112

Chapter 7 132

Chapter 8 150

Chapter 9 170

Chapter 10 186

Epilogue 207

Endorsements 217

PREFACE

In today's turbulent world, many are without hope. Trapped by despondency and futility, they've sought relief in drugs . . . drinking . . . violence . . . and other acts of rebellion, bringing harm to themselves and others. For anyone imprisoned by despair, *Five Years to Life* proves there is a way out of the darkness. You'll discover how to break the bonds of hopelessness, take responsibility for your situation, and learn about the unconditional love of your Heavenly Father.

ACKNOWLEDGEMENTS

By the time this book is published, it will be many years since I first started writing it. During that period, many people have helped me along the way. I must take the time to thank them.

Thanks to . . .

My father . . . he's my bud.

My mom and stepdad, who in different ways encouraged me to keep going . . . and they still do.

My brothers and sisters—Buddy, Tony, Murphy, Cynthia and Rhona. Thanks for your input. You, too, Joyce.

Elder Earl Walker, the first person to say, "Sam, you ought to write a book."

Lila Frazier, who helped me on the very first writing. I love you . . . and Laura, too.

Margaret Dawson, Deanna Faulkner, Janet West, Becky Barnes, Mercy Pono, Mendy Eslinger, Barbara White and Maxine Eckes—all helped through the years by typing the manuscript.

William Shedrick, the first person to put this book on computer.

My Sunday school teacher Mrs. Harding. I'm a sunbeam for Jesus.

The Rev. Robert and Norma Smallwood, for pointing me to Bethany University.

Krissy West and Rachel Rodriguez, who were young but quite helpful in putting pages together.

Darlene Bogle . . . what can I say?

Bob Woodford, who, though he is home with the Lord now, continued to ask, "Is this where you want to stay?"

My Aunts Effie and Annie Mae, who kept praying and believing God to change my life.

Mt. Hermon Christian Writers Conference—what a blessing!

Pastor Don Green, the man I want to be like "when I grow up" . . . caring.

My brother-in-law, Dwight.

Dennis Braudrick, whose life inspires me.

Elizabeth Sherrill—Ericka and I will never forget our time with you in New York. You are special.

My "goodest" buddy, Professor Arneson, who typed from my hieroglyphics.

My children—Royce, Ericka and Andre. You have encouraged me more than I could put into words.

I cannot forget those rejection notices. Boy, what a boost!

Last, "Thank You" to the Lord. You've given me so much. I pray this book brings much glory to You for what You have done in my life. I love You so much.

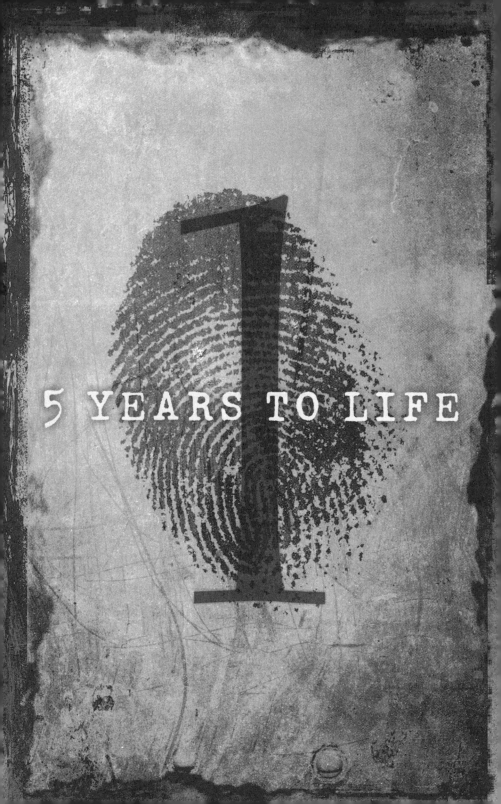

WHY WAS I BORN?
I DIDN'T ASK TO BE
HOW LONG WILL I LIVE?
ASK GOD
GOD, I NEED TO KNOW
WHY AM I BLACK?

Someone was banging on the front door. I yelled out from the bedroom, "Answer the stupid door!" More people, I figured, coming over to join the party. The party was over. I was in bed with a chick, not about to get up. I heard the door open. My cousin Shep's voice, then men's voices. One of them sounded like Officer Hank. At age 17 I was already well-acquainted with the small police force of Atwater, California. I jumped up and hid behind the door.

Someone was entering the bedroom, shining a flashlight on the bed, asking the chick if she had seen Sam Huddleston. She sat up clutching the blanket around her bare shoulders. "No, officer." The cop searched under the bed, looked in the closet, shined a light again on the bed and left. I stood on my toes behind the door, barely breathing. I hadn't done anything wrong. At least . . . nothing my booze-fogged brain could remember. But my instinctive reaction at the approach of police was to hide.

I wondered if the neighbors had complained about the

noise. This was one of the row of small two-family houses strung along Highway 99 across from the tracks. The other half of it was occupied by an elderly couple who didn't appreciate the constant partying. But why come looking for me? This was my older cousin's place. I lived two houses over, with my mom and her husband.

The officer returned. I felt the door jerk away, winced as the flashlight shone straight in my eyes. The cop jumped backward, dropping the torch. He picked it up quickly. "Come out in the living room."

In Shep's living room, I couldn't believe what I saw. There stood four policemen, two of them with shotguns. As I walked in they cocked the guns. "Sit down on the couch," said the cop who had followed me out of the bedroom. I sat on the cold plastic. What was wrong with these guys? They had picked me up lots of times—petty stuff—breaking and entering, suspicion of burglary, most recently for passing bad checks. How come this time they were acting like I was some kind of violent animal?

"Sam Huddleston?"

"What, uh, what you want, man?" I was so drugged on red devils, rum and beer I couldn't talk straight. "You have the right to remain silent," and he continued quoting me my rights.

"Yeah, yeah, I already know that crap, man."

"You're under arrest."

I laughed. "For what now?"

"Suspicion of robbery and attempted murder."

"For what?" I looked from one face to the other. "You guys are nuts! Get the hell out of here," I yelled. "You're always trying to pin something on me." I stumbled drunkenly to my feet. The officers with shotguns lowered the barrels and pointed them straight at me. Another officer pushed me back on the couch. "Sit there while I get your pants." I was wearing nothing but boxer shorts.

"I'll get my own pants. What time is it anyway?"

Someone answered, "Four-thirty."

I lurched to my feet again. The policeman placed his hand on my chest: "Sit down! I'll get them."

I pushed his hand away. "No, you won't, sucker! I'll get my own pants." I wobbled back into the bedroom and leaned down to pick up my Levis at the side of the bed. My fingers touched something damp and sticky. I was too drunk to have any idea what it was, I just knew I didn't want to put those pants on. I kicked them under the bed, went to the closet and grabbed a pair of my cousin's pants. It took a while to get into them. He was three sizes smaller than me and I never got them fastened. I pulled on a shirt and left it hanging down in front.

The girl in the bed asked, "What's wrong, Sammy? Why are the police here? Is the party over?"

Stupid broad, I thought. "Yep, it's over. Just go back to sleep," I said.

Before leaving the house I was handcuffed. Out on the street there must have been a half dozen police cars. What was going on? I was placed in the backseat of one of the squad cars. In the backyards roosters were starting to crow. Two houses down I saw my mom and stepfather coming out of their house to go fishing, their weekly Saturday ritual: leave by dawn, return after dark. I thought about all the times my stepfather had taken me fishing. I saw him look in the direction of the squad cars, then turn away. Visits by the police weren't that unusual in this neighborhood; don't get involved, we would tell each other. My stepdad opened the garage, backed up his car and began to hitch up the boat. He got back into the car and from the garage emerged his pride and joy, his 18-foot outboard with its 54-horsepower Johnson engine.

He got out again and closed the garage door. *They don't know I'm over here*, I thought. *They probably think I'm there in the house—in my own bedroom.* I leaned as near the window as the handcuffs would let me. "Mama! Mama!"

She started walking toward the police car. Two officers blocked her way. I could hear her asking, "Is that my son? Mike, is that you, baby?" Mama never called me Sam, always Mike, after my middle name, Michael.

"Sorry, ma'am," said one officer. "You can't talk to him."

"Mama, Mama," I yelled. "I didn't do it!" Those were always the first words out of my mouth when arrested: "I didn't do it!"

They drove me to the police station in Atwater and placed me in a holding cell. Mama arrived a few minutes later. *Boy,* I thought, *I've got more attention from her as a criminal than I ever did as a child.* All I could tell her was that I didn't know what was going on. I was still so high I could hardly talk.

They let Mama stay only five minutes. After she left I lay on the cot thinking. *Sam, you sure have a knack for keeping your butt in a sling!* I was already on house arrest on the bad check rap, due to start serving a six-months-to-one-year sentence next week at a camp for youthful nonviolent offenders.

"Sam, Sam, wake up!" The sergeant was shaking my shoulder. "The captain wants to see you."

I sat up groggily. *The captain? This is crazy!* I had never been through all this jive before. Normally I was arrested and either charged and taken to juvenile hall, or talked to and released. As I entered his office, the captain said, "Sit down, Sammy."

"What is, uh, going on?" My tongue felt stuck to the bottom of my mouth. "I'm tired of you guys always trying to, uh, put something on me."

"What do you mean, Sammy?"

"You know what I mean. Here I am in jail, for they say robbing somebody and, man, attempted murder, when I was at a party all night. Twenty people will tell you I never left the house."

Another officer entered the room and whispered something to the captain. The captain took off his glasses, and put them on again. "The first thing you need to know is . . .," he paused and inspected his glasses again. "Sam," he finally said, "it's not attempted murder anymore. It's murder. The man died on the operating table." He replaced his glasses and stared at me. "Don't you remember the liquor store you robbed last night?"

"Died! Who died? What liquor store?" Between the drugs and the drink, I could hardly remember who I was, much less last night. I started laughing. I knew this was a setup. They were trying to pin something on me, and I was not falling for it.

"Captain, it ain't gonna work. I ain't coppin' to nothin'."

The captain repeated his words, slowly. "Don't you remember last night?"

I sat there thinking, *Liquor store, what liquor store?* The whole past week I had stayed in a drunken stupor, trying not to think about the camp where I'd be going in a few days. I recalled taking a little money for booze from Mama's purse. But robbing a store? I knew I didn't do it. This time I was innocent. This time I didn't do it.

I opened my mouth to let out some smart remark when the fog in my brain lifted momentarily. Me leaving the party with Shep. "We're out of rum, man!" Going to get more. Shep was older—old enough to purchase alcohol. Getting in a car . . . whose car? Someone drove . . . can't remember. The liquor store. Only no one had any money.

Decided to rob the place. But how, with no gun? I had a knife. I gave it to Shep. "We'll just scare him." But the guy fights. Bottles flying past my head, breaking on the wall. I start to run, then turn back. Can't leave Shep. There's a cut on my forehead, blood dripping on my pants. Shep is screaming, "Look out, Sam! Snakes! Snakes'll bite you!" I look for the snakes. Then I see that Shep has freaked out.

Shep has the knife. He's stabbing at the guy, shouting, "Snakes! Snakes!"

The man's yelling, "Don't stab me anymore!"

"You mean . . . the guy died!" I reached for the trash can. I bent over it, vomiting and crying. Oh, hell, Sammy, oh, hell. Not me. I'm not mixed up in anything like this. My dad is a Sunday school superintendent. My grandfather is a deputy sheriff. I can't have been involved in someone's actually dying.

I couldn't stop vomiting. I was screaming, "No, no!"

"Settle down, Sam, settle down." Two officers ran into the room, guns drawn, but all they saw was a kid bent over a trashcan puking out his guts. This is not the way it's supposed to happen. Me and Shep only had a few pills and some booze. At school, where I started doing drugs and alcohol, they said, "It won't hurt you." They said it made you feel good, helped you enjoy life. Someone lied. Surely those pills didn't cause me to lose control to the point that I . . . This was all a bad dream. I knew I would wake up soon.

I did wake up and nothing had changed. An old buddy,

George, had apparently snitched on Shep and me. Because of the severity of the crime, I was to be tried as an adult. I was taken to the county jail in Merced, six miles from Atwater. Shep had been arrested, too, but I didn't know whether he was in Merced or somewhere else.

The cell in Merced was dark and cold, with no window and only one tiny light bulb in the ceiling. The toilet and sink were made of a single piece of aluminum and the steel bunk bed was bolted to the wall. I lay on my back on the bunk. Three days had passed since my arrest, and my mind had started to clear. I stared at the overhead bulb and thought back over seventeen years. I sure didn't want to dwell on the future.

In my mind I went back to the days before Mama went away, when we were all together as a family in Livingston. Livingston was a real small town, only three or four thousand people, eight miles on the other side of Atwater. There were six kids in our family—four boys, two girls. The oldest was Buddy Ray. He was the joker of the family, always clowning.

Then me. I was a year younger than Buddy. Every year for three days we celebrate being the same age. Then came Tony, two years after me. He was the best athlete in the family. Even as a little guy he had a lot of speed. Seventeen months after Tony came Murphy. His hardship was he stuttered. We three older boys teased him for that, except when Daddy was around. Following Murphy came the girls, Cynthia and Rhona. Cynthia's nickname was "Red" because of the color of her hair. Rhona's was "Lois Lane"—she told it all. By the time Mama was 25 she had given birth six times. Her mother, whom we all called

Mother Carrie, lived with us, too. She dipped snuff and chewed tobacco.

We were an athletic family who played a lot of baseball together. I always enjoyed it when Mama would play with us. In those days, of course, before Mama went away, my sisters were too young to play. Mama would come up to the plate, roll up the pant legs of her jeans and swing the bat. Mama was always laughing. Whether she hit the ball or missed it, she'd be laughing. Even as she ran the bases, she would laugh. She ran fast. We were all yelling, "Throw the ball to me! Throw the ball to me!" Everybody wanted to tag Mama out. Being pigeon-toed and bowlegged, I could never catch her. Buddy and Tony were the only ones speedy enough.

When she would run those bases, I used to smile, thinking, *That's my mama.* It was great for a little boy to be able to play with the person he loved the most.

When Daddy played he never hit his hardest, or we would never have found the ball. Daddy was muscular, a football and baseball star back in his high school days. If we weren't playing baseball, we would go swimming in one of the nearby canals. Daddy would toss me and my brothers high in the air and we would hit the water with a splash. I'd come up out of the water and he'd pick me up again and give me a squeeze. He was always giving us bear hugs. His big arms and muscular physique made him the biggest man in my world.

The San Joaquin Valley was a wonderful place. Fruit and nut trees—peaches, plums, nectarines, cherries, almonds, walnuts—vineyards and melon fields crisscrossed by canals flowing with blue run-off water from the snow-covered Sierra Nevada Mountains. Most of the vineyards belonged to the Gallo Winery. There was also a small chicken processing plant in Livingston, where Mama worked. She used to clean people's houses, too, until one of the employer's children called her a nigger as she scrubbed their floor. I recalled her telling us, "I have to clean houses to help pay the bills, but I don't have to work for folks who call me a nigger."

Daddy didn't want her working at all. He said it was his responsibility to support his family. He felt his job as a janitor at the high school brought in enough. "Lee"—Daddy always called Mama by her middle name—"you don't have to work."

"But Edward, I want to work."

"Okay, but you don't have to."

"I know, honey." She kept working.

There were only half a dozen black families in Livingston and racial incidents were rare; nevertheless, both my parents were sensitive to the subject. I remembered an episode in Livingston's little community park. As the family piled into the car after a ballgame, a man called after Daddy, "See you later, Sunshine." For a moment Daddy just sat quietly behind the wheel. Then he pulled the car up to where the man was standing.

"Mister," Daddy said, "my name is Edward Ray Huddleston, Senior. You can call me any of those names you choose but don't you ever call me Sunshine again."

He put the car in reverse and drove off.

My mama loved scary movies on TV. Some nights she would let me stay up late and watch with her. I never looked at the screen—the stories gave me nightmares. I would sit at my mama's feet with my arms wrapped around her smooth, pretty legs as she sat in front of our black-and-white set in the old overstuffed chair. She kept a blanket over the chair to keep the stuffing from getting on her clothes. Mama sat there watching the TV and I sat there watching her.

I loved being alone with her, just me and my mama. During the day I could never manage it. It was difficult to get individual attention from her with six kids clamoring to be cared for.

Lying in that jail cell in Merced, I recalled the happiest moment of my life. It was late one night and I was crying because I was afraid the bogeyman was going to get me. The big old house we lived in was scary. It sat in a big field with twisted old olive trees around it and an archway covered with vines out front.

My brothers and I shared the same twin-bedded room, two of us per bed. Across the hall was my parents' room.

"Mama," I called softly, not wanting to wake up my brothers.

"Yeah, baby?"

"Can I come and get in bed with you and Daddy?"

"No, Sammy, go to sleep," came Daddy's sleepy voice.

"But I'm scared."

"Of what, baby?"

"The bogeyman. I know he's going to get me."

"Boy, go to sleep. Don't nobody want you except your mother and me, and we're having second thoughts."

"Please, Daddy!"

"He's really frightened, Edward," I heard Mama say.

"Sure, baby, you can come in here with us."

"Will you come get me, Mama?"

"No," Daddy answered for her. "If you want to come in our room, you have to come by yourself. Nobody's coming to get you."

"Okay, then. Here I come. Are you ready? Well, here I come. Okay, I'm coming. I'm gettin' ready. Here I come." I jumped out of the bed, raced into the dark hallway and smack into the open door of the hall cupboard. I fell to the floor, scrambled screaming to my feet, ran into my parents' room and dove into the bed, knees first. I snuggled between my parents and lay there sobbing with relief. Though it was pitch-dark, I was safe now. The bogeyman would never come into this room. And if he did, my daddy would get him. My whole world was perfect. I was with my mama and daddy. Nothing could hurt me.

The next morning when I woke up Daddy had gone to work. He had started a gardening business in addition to his janitor job. Mama was still asleep. I lay there looking at the smile on her face. She was always smiling and ever so pretty with curly shoulder-length black hair and long, curling lashes. When she woke up I pretended to be asleep and she started to tickle me. My brothers and sisters heard us and came running into the room. "How come Sammy got to sleep with you and Daddy, Mama?"

"Yeah, how come?" I sat up, hugged my mama and smiled.

Daddy started taking Buddy and me to work with him when he cut lawns, and to the high school to help him there. We would push the mowers, pull weeds, sweep sidewalks. I liked working with Daddy. Even better I like helping Mama with the housework. As a family we went to church both Sunday and midweek. Daddy was Sunday school superintendent and we boys joined Royal Ambassadors. I earned a New Testament for memorizing John 3:16: "For God so loved the world, that he gave his only begotten Son, that whosoever believeth in him should not perish, but have everlasting life." I didn't know what it meant but I had it word-perfect.

One day Daddy came home from work real proud. "Lee, I'm going to be a deacon!" he told Mama.

"A what?"

"A deacon."

She wasn't smiling. "First you became a Christian," she told him. "Then you came home and announced that, since you had gotten religion, we all were going to get religion. You stopped me from seeing my friends. I can't drink a little wine for my anemia, I can't get away from these kids for a few days to give my nerves some rest. You say all I need to do is read the Bible. You force me to go to church, even if I don't want to. Now you come home telling me you're going to be a deacon, and I'm supposed to be glad?"

After that I noticed Mama didn't play with us kids as much. The biggest change was she quit laughing and smiling, and she yelled a lot.

Late one night Mama put all six of us kids into our little two-door Simca. Murphy asked, "Where we g-g-goin', Mama?"

"To Los Angeles."

"Oh, boy!" We all began to cheer. Going on a trip! I was 8, old enough to read the freeway signs: "Los Angeles, 280 miles."

When we got to Los Angeles, though, we stayed only one day. Then we drove back north. Only we didn't stop in Livingston. Mama kept right on driving clear up to Oakland, a hundred miles farther. It was cramped in the car and we were all hot and cranky. In Oakland we went to some relative's house. We had barely arrived when Daddy pulled up. We kids ran out to greet him. He didn't smile. He kept asking, "Where's your mama?" He went in the house while we waited outside.

A few minutes later, we kids were on our way back to
Livingston with Daddy. All of us were crying because
we had left Mama standing in the doorway. None of us
had any idea what was going on. A few days later Mama
came home. But we didn't play ball or go swimming.
Mama wouldn't let me watch late movies with her either.
I woke up early one morning and went into my parents'
bedroom. It was empty. Daddy always went to work early,
but where was Mama? I looked all over the house. I asked
Mama Carrie, "Where's Mama?"

"She's gone, baby."

"Where?"

"She's just gone."

"When's she comin' back?"

"She's gone, baby, just gone." Mama Carrie pulled me
close and started to cry. I just stood there trying to figure
out how my mother could be gone and what we had done
to make her leave.

Each day I would come home from school and sit in the
front yard, looking down the road hoping Mama would
come home. At last one day, this big, brown convertible
pulled up into the front yard. It was Mama. As soon as
she stepped out of the car, she was smothered by us kids.
I found me a leg and held on. *We're a family again. My
mama's home.*

Tony ran to get Daddy. He came out and we kids got
quiet. Daddy walked up to Mama. They hugged and

kissed. We kids began to jump and yell. I kept thinking, *Everything is all right now, everything is all right.*

A few days later, Mama started packing some clothes. "Where you going, Mama?"

"What, baby?" She looked as though she had been crying.

"Where are you going?"

"Back to where I was at. I'm going back to Los Angeles."

"But Mama, this is your house."

"Not anymore, honey. Not anymore."

"Mama, Mama, you can't leave us again! We love you!"

"I love you, too, baby, but I've got to go." She took her suitcase to her car and I was following all the way.

"Mama?"

"Yeah, baby?"

"Can I go with you? Please, Mama, take me. Take me with you. I'll be good! I promise I'll be good. Please, please." Now she was crying, too.

"Baby, you don't understand. You can't go." She went back to the house for her other suitcase. I jumped into the trunk of the brown convertible and pulled a blanket over

me. Daddy came out of the house and dragged me from
the trunk. I kicked and yelled as my mama pulled out of
the driveway in that new convertible.

"Mama, please don't leave!" My brothers and sisters
were yelling as loudly as I was. Everybody was crying—
Mama Carrie and Daddy, too. Everybody was crying.
When Daddy let me go, I ran after the car, but it was too
late. I stood and watched the car disappear down the road
between the peach trees and watermelon field. She was
gone. I walked slowly back home, went into the grape
field behind our house and cried and cried and cried.
When I finished crying I began to hit the dirt. Over and
over again I said, "Ain't nobody ever going to hurt me like
that again. Nobody is ever going to hurt me again."

Two years passed. We wrote letters and sometimes
Mama wrote back. She mentioned in one that she had
met this guy named John. A few months later she wrote
that they were married. Her new last name was Akins.
Married? When did she and Daddy get a divorce? How
come no one told us?

Mama Carrie got a picture of Mama and her new
husband. He had a dark complexion and wore his hair in
an Afro. He had a big smile. I would have been smiling,
too, if I were standing with my mama. His belly stuck
out. Two things about him looked okay, though. He
was holding a cigarette and it looked like one of his feet
pointed in, like mine.

Sundays after church we would visit Daddy's parents in
Merced. Daddy Bryce Huddleston and Mama Susie had
their yard fixed for their grandchildren. Swings, monkey

bars, a huge slide and plenty of green grass to run on barefoot. I loved to feel the blades of grass under my feet.

Daddy's family had migrated from Muskogee, Oklahoma, in the 1930s. Daddy Bryce collected and sold scrap iron. He also worked in the fields during harvest season.

Daddy Bryce was a handsome man. I seldom saw him without a Stetson hat except when he was wearing his county sheriff's uniform.

To augment his income, he also gave haircuts. Many times he would cut us boys' hair. "Son," he began one day as he wrapped the towel around my neck, "what's your last name?"

"Huddleston, Daddy Bryce."

"That's right, and don't ever forget it. You're a Huddleston. Be proud, walk proud and never bring shame to that name."

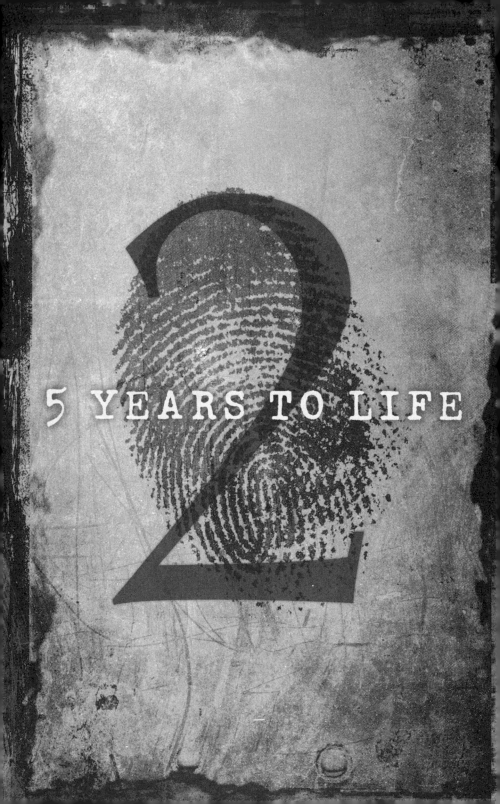

RUNNING, NO ONE UNDERSTANDS RUNNING IS THE KEY RUNNING TO FIND HAPPINESS RUNNING . . . FROM ME

Many nights as we were almost asleep Daddy would come into our room.

"Boys, boys."

"Yes, sir?" one of us would respond.

"Did you boys pray for your mama?"

"No, sir."

"Then get up and pray for her."

All four of us would get up, kneel beside our beds, in our underwear, and pray.

"Dear Lord," one of us would say.

"Dear Lord," the others would echo.

"Please watch over our mama."

"Please watch over our mama."

"We don't know where she's at. . . ."

"Save her Lord. . . ."

"Before it's too late. Amen."

"Boys, you know I love you very much."

"We love you too, Daddy."

Many nights as I lay in bed asleep I was awakened by someone kneeling beside the bed. I would roll over to see who it was . . . Daddy. He'd be praying.

On winter mornings before school Daddy took us boys with him to one of the neighboring fields to pick up anything the tractors had left after harvesting. The corn and sweet potatoes made good eating for the hogs we raised, out back of the house. Daddy knew the farmers and had their permission.

It was also an opportunity to impress on us his philosophy of hard work. "Sammy," Daddy said one morning.

"Sir?"

"How come you and Buddy are just standing there with your hands folded?"

"'Cause we're cold, Daddy."

"You know why?"

"Yes, sir. All this fog and frost on the . . ."

"No. It's because you're not working. Now grab some of them sweet potatoes and throw them in the back of the truck."

Our truck was an old flatbed 1947 Dodge with a red cab. The only thing that made going into the fields fun was that Daddy let us take turns steering it. He would put it in a low gear and it would move slowly down the field. The driver's job was to keep it going straight. Besides, you could stay warm by the heat that came off the pipes through the holes in the floorboard.

One day after school we were gleaning corn in a field when a car pulled up. A white man with a beard rolled down the window and yelled out.

"Say, you Eddie Huddleston?"

"Sure am," said Daddy.

"Could I speak to you a moment?"

"Sure." We kids tried to get close to listen but Daddy chased us off. After a while the car drove away and he called us over.

"You boys know who that was?"

"No, sir."

"He was from the welfare office."

"What's 'welfare,' Daddy?"

"They help poor and needy people—give them food and money."

"Are they gonna help us?" Tony asked.

"He wanted to."

"What they g-gonna g-g-give us?" Murphy stammered.

"Nothing, boys. Not now. Not ever."

"How come?" asked Buddy.

"We're poor but we're not needy. My daddy raised me to work hard and I'm gonna raise you boys the same." Then he said some words I never forgot: "Never let anyone do for you what you can do for yourself.

"You boys listen and listen good. Welfare is a good thing for folks who can't help themselves. But I told the man, 'I don't know who told you I needed help with my six kids. If I couldn't support them, I shouldn't have had them.' Boys, as long as God gives you good health and strength, that's all the welfare you need. You know that big family down the street from us?"

"Yes, sir?"

"Well, they're on welfare. The father got sick. But now he's well and the family is still on welfare. They're raising their young'uns to believe they don't have to do their best in school. Welfare will take care of them. That's all wrong.

In this family we pay our own way. We work hard and stick together. You boys hear me? We stick together."

On hot summer days Daddy woke us up early.

"Daddy, it's still dark out there. We can't cut lawns in the dark."

"It won't be dark for long." He had breakfast on the table—fried chicken, rice and gravy, cornbread, spaghetti.

"Eat hearty, boys, we've got a lot of yards to do today." We ate up, loaded the truck with tools, and off we'd go—all summer long, all day, six days a week.

In the evenings we played baseball on the summer league team. Buddy pitched and I caught. Daddy gave us a quarter for every base hit, and a dollar for a home run. I got a dollar for triples. Daddy said because of my feet and slow running, a triple for me was like a homer for someone else.

Mama Carrie taught Buddy and me to cook and clean house. She made us mop the floor on our knees with a rag. If it wasn't clean, we had to do it again. She would tell us, "If it's worth doing, it's worth doing right."

"Sammy."

"Yes, Mama Carrie?"

"Come here and sit down, boy. I'm going to teach you to sew."

"I don't want to sew."

"Yes, you do. You boys aren't going to grow up depending on a lady to do everything for you. Here's a needle. Now thread it."

I was a freshman in high school now, which meant I could play football and high school baseball. I was already familiar with the rooms at the high school, having cleaned most of them with Daddy. During my freshman year, Daddy started dating a lady named Flossie. Her black hair was streaked with gray and she was real tall—the same height as Daddy. She seemed to like us kids. I hoped so 'cause there were a bunch of us. She had none of her own. She called everybody "sweetie" and had a big smile that revealed the gap between her two front teeth.

"Doll" (Flossie's nickname) started going to church with us. She had a beautiful voice; she sang solos in church when someone requested it.

Daddy was around her so much I became resentful. I felt she was trying to take Mama's place. I didn't want her around. She tried winning me over with her hugs and kisses but there was only one woman I wanted to hug and kiss me and she wasn't it.

With Doll around most of the time, Mother Carrie moved out. I felt deserted again. Another woman I let myself love, and she walked out, too. She went to stay with Mama and John who were living in Delhi, six miles away. Mama and John came to our church sometimes. Every Sunday morning the pastor called for those wanting prayer to come down front. Daddy always got us kids to go and stand together as a family for prayer.

Mama started coming up front, too, for altar prayer with her new husband. Sure enough, his left foot turned in, just like mine. I stood with my brothers and sisters and looked at Mama standing on the other side of the aisle. Each Sunday I moved closer and closer toward her until one morning I stood right beside her. After a while I felt her hands on my shoulder. I looked quickly at Daddy. He was staring at me kind of funny.

Daddy was offered a position at another church as Sunday school superintendent. So we left. God and church had again separated me from my mother. Daddy married Doll.

Being a freshman was tough. The word around school was if you didn't drink sloe gin, you weren't "cool." After every football game some of the guys on the team went out drinking. The guys kept telling me that I didn't know what I was missing. My curiosity rose. I wondered what sloe gin tasted like. Everybody else was doing it, so it must be all right.

One Friday night I stayed at the high school. I belonged to F.F.A. (Future Farmers of America) and we were putting on a small tractor show on the school ballfield. Someone had to spend the night watching the equipment. I asked Daddy and he said okay.

Instead of watching the tractors, though, some of us went riding around with Gabe. He was older and possessed something no one else had . . . wheels.

"Hey, Gabe," someone said. "Why don't we get some sloe gin and beer?"

"You guys got some bread?"

"Sure, man."

"Okay, then," Gabe agreed.

He drove to the liquor store downtown. We all gave him some money. A few minutes later, he came out with a bottle of sloe gin and a six-pack of Colt .45 beer. We drove out into the country to a swimming hole called Solomon's Drop. Gabe stopped, turned up the music on the radio, and we got out of the car. Gabe opened a beer and passed it to me. I had never tasted beer in my life. I didn't know what to expect. I was afraid Daddy would find out, afraid that I'd get caught and get kicked off the football team.

The thought came to me: *Sammy, go home. You can walk. Leave, Sam.* Instead I just stood there staring into the dark, starry sky.

This is my life, I thought. *It only affects me, and Daddy'll never know.* I took a big gulp out of the can. Yuk! I had never tasted anything so awful in all my life.

"Hey, Sam, try the gin."

"Sure, pass it here." I had gone this far.

I turned up the bottle and started swallowing. "Hey, hey, take it easy. Save some for the rest of us!" I finished a whole can of Colt .45 and four or five drinks of sloe gin. I could hardly stand, let alone walk back to the car. "Better take him home," someone said.

"No, no. Take me to Delhi. My mother lives there."

"Where?"

"On Bloss Avenue."

They half carried me to the car. At Mama's, they propped me against the front door, rang the doorbell and drove off in a hurry. When Mama opened the door I fell in. She yelled for John and they dragged me inside and put me on the couch.

The room started spinning. I jumped up and ran for the door. Something inside my stomach was trying to get out through my mouth. I never made it to the door. I threw up on my mom's rug, then fell face-first into it. "O God," I moaned, "make this room hold still and I promise I'll never do this again." A prayer I would make—and break—many times in the next few years.

The next morning I wished I had never heard of beer and gin. But I went to school and did like everyone else. "Man," I told my friends, "you've got to drink some sloe gin, it's great."

"Did you get sick, Sam?"

"Hell, no, man. Just mellow, baby."

I started to resent living at home. I found out I could get

away with much more at Mama's. She never told Daddy about my being drunk almost every time I went to see her. She let me light her cigarettes. She let me and my friends listen to rock 'n' roll music. She let us dance and even danced with us. I began to wonder what it would be like to live with her and John and decided to ask Daddy. If he said yes, I'd have my own bedroom for the first time in my life.

"Daddy, uh, I've been thinking."

"About what, Sammy?"

"About how crowded it is here."

"Yes, it's crowded, all right. Do you have a solution?"

"Uh-huh."

"Well, what is it?"

"Me, uh, me going to live with Mama."

He gave me that funny look again. "Sammy, I'm only going to say this once. All these years we've been a family. We've stuck together through thick and thin. More thin than thick. You're 14 now. In four or five years you'll be leaving home anyway. Until then, this is where you stay."

I said, "Okay," and walked away. But inside I was furious. Who did he think he was, telling me I couldn't live with my own mother?

I didn't want to wait five years. I wanted my

independence now. I started going to Mama's after school several times a week. When Daddy asked where I had been, I lied. Then I met this guy in school and we became quick friends . . . too quick.

"Sammy."

"Yeah, man?"

"Let's go and steal some stuff from a store."

I just laughed. "What for?"

"For kicks."

I was bored, so we did. We got caught. Daddy found out and I got the belt.

But my friend was right: Stealing was exciting. I kept on doing it. It had been six months since my talk with Daddy about living with Mama. I knew I'd never get his permission. I began to think about running away. Some of the kids in school were doing it. The girl who lived next door to us was always fighting with her mother. I could hear them from our house. At school, she told me how much she hated her family and wanted to run away. Run away . . . her, too.

"L.A. I have some friends there."

"Hey, so do I." My aunt was in Los Angeles.

"Why don't we run off together?"

"Let me think about it."

We had these talks daily. Could this be my answer? I lay awake at night and thought about it. I had $65 in a savings account Daddy made me open. That would cover bus fare with some left over.

One day I went grocery shopping with Daddy. As he filled the shopping cart, I walked over to the fresh fruit department. When I thought no one was looking I grabbed a pear, took two big bites, turned it upside-down and put it back.

Before I could swallow, someone tapped me on the shoulder. I turned around. It was Daddy.

"Sammy, did you pick up a piece of fruit?"

My mouth was full so I shook my head, no.

"Are you sure?"

Again I shook my head.

"What's that juice running from your mouth?"

He picked up the pear and turned it over. "Did you do this?" Swallowing, I managed a throaty, "No, sir."

"Boy, I ought to take my belt off right here. You're lying, Sammy, and it's not the first time. You're getting it when we get home. You're dragging down the Huddleston name. Livingston's a small town and there are no secrets."

Boy, did I get it when we got home. When he left me crying in the bedroom, I made up my mind this was my last licking.

That week I withdrew my funds from the bank, packed some clothes and called Sara. I told her that I was going to L.A. She wanted to go, too. I got Gabe to drive us to the bus station in Merced.

As the bus pulled onto the freeway, I started thinking about the note I had left Daddy:

Dear Daddy,

I'm running away. You won't find me. I know you don't love me. You never did, because I look so much like Mama. Don't try to find me. You won't. Besides, I'd rather go to juvenile hall than to live in your house anymore.

Later, old man

I should never have left that note! What am I doing? This is crazy. What about Buddy . . . Tony . . . Murphy . . . Cynthia . . . Rhona? What about me? Shoot, I'm getting off this bus and going home. I know I've got problems, but none so big that Daddy and I can't work them out.

I stood up.

"Where are you going, Sammy?"

"To talk to the bus driver."

"About what?"

"Uh . . . about where the restroom is."

"It's right there." Sara pointed to a small door at the rear.

"Oh, thanks."

That night on the bus I got drunk again. I had stolen some sloe gin from the liquor store in Livingston. In L.A. I called my aunt and she came to pick us up.

She didn't act surprised when she found out I was drinking. Sara and I gave her some money and she bought us some Old English 800 malt beer. I got drunk, and this time I passed out.

I was awakened by someone crying. Someone's face was on my back, crying. I jumped up and turned around. It was Mama. How did she get here? How long had I been out? Delhi was 300 miles away. Boy, was I glad to see her. But at the same time, I wouldn't reach out to her. I remembered when she left, and I was the one crying. It was a weird feeling but I sort of liked seeing her cry for a change.

Four days later Sara and Mama and I were on a bus heading north. Sara was going home and I was going to live with Mama in Delhi. It was funny, though—all I could think about was my brothers and sisters. I recalled all the good times we had when we were younger. I remembered how Buddy and Tony would get me down on the ground and tickle me. I remembered gleaning corn and sweet potatoes for the hogs . . . and the big breakfasts Daddy would have waiting when we woke up. How when we were little he'd toss us high in the air.

The closer we got to Livingston the more I wanted to go home. I didn't want to live with my mother. I looked at her in the seat behind me and she was smiling from ear to ear. It seemed as though my going to live with her made her happy. Each time I turned around she smiled more. I was tempted at one point to ask her to quit smiling. Seeing Daddy and the others was all I thought about. But how could I hurt Mama? She was all hyped up because I was going to live with her—the only one of her six children who wanted to. The bus pulled up to the blue-and-white terminal building in Merced with the Greyhound dog in lights out front. Sara's folks were there, and so was Mama's husband, John. He took Mama's suitcase and I followed them to the car.

The Livingston high school served Delhi, too, so the next day I saw Buddy in the corridor.

"Sammy, why did you leave?"

"Man, Buddy, I'm tired of living with Daddy."

"Tired? Tired?" he yelled.

"Yeah, tired."

"Suppose Daddy had gotten tired of us! Where would we be now?

"I know, I know. But I'm going to live with Mama."

"You're stupid, man. You've got problems . . . big ones."

School was no longer fun. The teachers all knew Daddy and word got around that I had left home. As Daddy said, there are no secrets in a small town. I was booted off the freshman baseball team. I had missed two practices while I was in L.A., but I suspected that wasn't the whole reason.

Yet there was someone whose feelings hadn't changed. Daddy. He was home the day Mama took me to get my clothes.

"Hi, Daddy." Oh, how I wanted to tell him I was home to stay! I wanted to tell him that I was sorry and had made a terrible mistake. But I didn't.

"May I talk to you for a moment, Sammy?"

"Sure."

"I got the note you left me when you ran away." He held up the sheet of lined school writing paper. "I want you to know that it hit me deeply. I also want you to know that I don't believe you meant what you said. I'm keeping this note, and one day we'll burn it together.

"We want you back home, Sammy. I'm sorry you think there wasn't enough love to keep you here. I know we have house rules that you'll have to obey, but rules are everywhere. In fact, it's the rules that have kept our family together. Meanwhile, Sammy, I feel sorry for you. You've got a long, hard row to hoe unless you surrender your life to Jesus soon."

There he went with that "Jesus talk" again—the kind of talk that drove Mama away, that broke up our home.

"Do you want to stay with your mother, Sammy?"

Silence. We looked eye to eye. The moment of truth. Would I listen to my true feelings, or to the voice that kept saying *Run, run*? "Yes, Daddy," I said, knowing it wasn't true. "I do."

"Very well. You've made your decision. But remember this. You're always welcome home. If you're somewhere and haven't the money to get home, call and I'll come get you. You may not live with me, but"—silence as still as death broke into his speech—"you're still my son. I love you now and always will."

All the way back to Delhi in the car with Mama, those words echoed in my head:

"You're still my son."

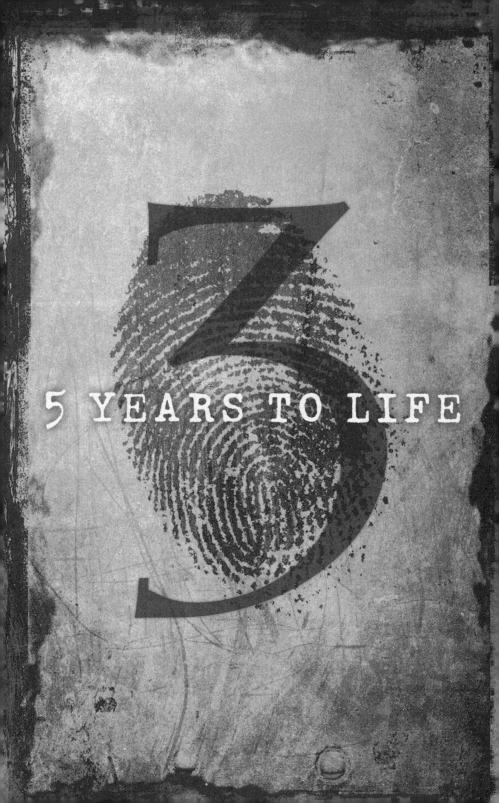

IN LIFE, AT DIFFERENT TIMES I NEARLY GAVE UP HOPE BUT EVERY TIME I DID HERE CAME THIS PIECE OF ROPE

At Mama's I had my own bedroom. My own bed, dresser and closet with only *my* clothes that I didn't have to share. My own window and my own door. All right! *This is freedom,* I thought as I sat on my bed blowing smoke rings. Mama didn't say anything about my smoking. There wasn't much she could say; she and John both smoked. Even Mama Carrie didn't say much; she chewed tobacco, which was the same thing.

At first I got along okay with my stepfather, too. I couldn't call John "Daddy," but I started calling him "Dad," which he dug a lot. He would take me fishing and bring along a beer for me, too.

One evening as I sat on my bed blowing rings, there was a rap on the window. I looked out and saw David from next door. David was a senior in high school.

"Come on, Sam. Let's take a walk."

We walked a couple of blocks, away from the houses.

"Sam, have you ever smoked marijuana?"

"Who, me? No way, man!" I turned to leave.

"Wait a minute, man, don't get so uptight."

"No way," I repeated. "I've heard it can really mess you up."

"Ah, you've been watching those films in school. That's all lies. Man, there's nothing like smoking pot! It makes you feel fantastic. You can handle it."

David lit a small, rolled-up cigarette, inhaled the smoke, then passed it to me. I noticed he held the smoke in so I did the same thing.

"How do you feel?"

"Okay, I guess. A little dizzy."

He lit up another one and I puffed on it. All of a sudden, I started feeling weird. My body felt numb and everything went out of focus.

David started laughing at me. He laughed and laughed and laughed. All I wanted to do was get back to my bedroom, but I couldn't feel my feet and legs. I stood there and cried, begging David to take me home. I thought David laughed before, but when he saw me crying, he about died laughing. He was rolling all over the sandy ground. The more I cried the more he laughed.

I don't remember how I got home. The next thing I

knew, it was morning. I sat up in bed thinking I had had a bad dream. At the bus stop, I saw David. He looked at me and started to laugh and then I knew it was no dream.

That experience should have soured me on pot, but David kept coming over, rolling cigarettes for me. One day I went to his house and asked for some. "You like it, huh, Sam?"

"Yeah, man, you got some more?"

"Sure. You got some bread?"

"You never charged me before."

"You never liked it before." I started buying ten-dollar bags from David. Since I wasn't weeding and mowing lawns with Daddy anymore, I had no income. Instead of stealing for the excitement of it, I began to steal to get money. I would go into my mother's purse, gym lockers at school and even Mama Carrie's handbag when it was open and she had her back turned. I started taking red devils, too—red-colored capsules that gave an instant high. I couldn't believe the changes that I was going through. I didn't even feel like the same person anymore.

I liked getting high, because thoughts of my brothers and sisters didn't hound me then.

When I wasn't high on drugs I was miserable, thinking of my lifestyle and the people I was hurting. I started to hate living with Mama. My escape was to use more drugs and drink more booze. I went to a friend's house after school and always came home late, past the curfew Mama and Dad had given me.

Dad began to get on my case about it. He wasn't my father. Who did he think he was, telling me what to do?

One night I stumbled into the house at half past one. I always tripped over the top step coming in, because it was higher than the rest. Dad was sitting in a chair drinking beer and watching TV.

I regained my balance and headed for my bedroom.

"I thought I told you to be home before midnight. You've got school tomorrow."

I kept walking. I was too drunk to listen to this crap.

"Hey, boy, don't you hear me talking to you?"

Boy? I ain't his boy!

I had reached the bedroom door when he grabbed me by the shoulder and spun me around. I swung at him and missed. He threw me down and pinned me to the floor, all 225 pounds of him.

"Listen, boy . . .," he began.

I started cussing. "Get off me, you big, black nigger!"

Mama came running into the living room. "John, get off him! Get off my baby!"

It was the first time we fought. Pretty soon it seemed that every time I drank, Dad and I ended up in a fistfight.

That year I also learned about sex. I was 15 now; Ann was 16. She started sneaking over late at night, and I let her into my bedroom through the window. Sex became like drugs . . . a habit.

Ann's father got suspicious and many nights she wasn't able to come. When that happened I looked for other action. One night I stole my stepfather's car. I was too young to have a license, but I had learned to drive handling Daddy's red truck in the fields. I got the keys off the dining room table, picked up three of my friends and we went cruising, 20 miles down to Merced.

The gas gauge got below empty and I pulled into a service station and told the attendant to fill it up. Then we found out no one had any money. I turned the motor back on and watched the attendant through the rearview mirror. When he pulled the gas nozzle out, I slammed the car into drive and drove off. The guy ran after us shouting, "Come back!" We started laughing.

We were five miles away, still laughing, when I saw flashing red lights coming up behind us. The guy had written down the license number.

The siren started going and I pulled over.

"All right, you guys up there, be totally still," came the voice over the speaker from the top of the cop car. "Don't anyone move."

Three other police cars pulled up behind that one. My
door was opened and I was pulled out and thrown to the
ground. I couldn't see the other guys but I knew they, too,
were getting a nose full of asphalt. The cop put his knee
in my back. I yelled out, "You're hurting me." He dug his
knee in harder. Then he snapped on handcuffs and jerked
me to my feet.

"All right, punk. What's your name?"

I kept silent.

He took my wallet from my back pocket and pulled out
my school ID card. His voice changed.

"'Samuel Huddleston.' Is that you?"

"Yeah."

"Are you related to Bryce Huddleston?"

"He's my grandfather."

"Say, fellas, this here's Bryce Huddleston's grandson."

The whole atmosphere changed on account of my
grandfather, a respected deputy sheriff. Though the cuffs
stayed on, the officers dusted off my shirt. I was placed in
the back of a police car and driven to Juvenile Hall. Since
they were over 18, my friends were taken to jail.

At the jail the cuffs were taken off and the officers left. A
big, fat white woman came in and told me to take off all

my clothes except my undershorts. She gave me a pair of white overalls.

"So your name is Samuel?"

"Yes, ma'am."

"This your first time here?"

"Yes, ma'am."

"Well, Samuel, I hope it's your last."

Not half as much as I did. I walked ahead of her down a corridor with concrete walls. There were rooms all along one side. Each had a solid steel door with a small window in it. There was a strong smell of disinfectant. We got to the last cell at the end of the hall. She opened the door. "You have a guest," she said to someone inside. She locked the door behind me and left. I could hear her footsteps as she walked back down the corridor, then the clang of the door that led back to the reception area.

I stood there scared.

"My name's Chunky," came the voice from the top bunk.

"What's yours?"

"Sam. Sam Huddleston."

"You can have the bottom bunk."

"Thanks."

I took off the overalls and sat on the edge of the bunkbed. There was a window in the wall with bars in it. The moon was bright—I could see a white porcelain toilet and sink. The concrete floor was cold beneath my bare feet.

"You been to the hall before, Sam?"

"No, man. First time."

"You scared?"

"A little," I lied. I was scared a lot.

"You want company?"

What was he talking about? There were two of us in a room the size of a closet.

"Why you scared, Sammy?" He climbed down from his bed and sat with me on the edge of mine. He sure was a big dude. In the moonlight I could see a scar clear down his right cheek. He wore a big, bushy Afro. He moved closer and I really got scared.

"How old are you, Sammy?"

"Seventeen," I said, adding two years and trying to deepen my voice.

"I'm 18," he said. "I told them 17 and the stupid cops believed me." His hand was moving while he talked. I shoved it away and jumped up.

He got up, too, a head taller than me. He hit me in the face.

I swung back but I knew I didn't hurt him. He kept hitting me. In the stomach, chest, groin. I tried to fight back but he was huge. No wonder they called him Chunky.

I started to yell but he said if I shouted again he would kill me. "I'm in here for shooting someone. Breaking your neck won't bother me a bit." I began to cry. I had heard about what was going to happen but never thought it would happen to *me*. I never thought I'd ever be raped by a guy.

Afterward I lay awake all night, crying and staring at the top bunk, planning how I would kill him. I also knew I'd never act on it and . . . that I could never, ever tell anyone.

The next morning a man opened the cell door. "Huddleston, grab your stuff. You're going home." I was so sore all over I could hardly walk. Chunky sat up in his bunk and watched me go.

In the reception room Mama was waiting. She reached out to hug me and I jumped back about a mile. I didn't want anybody touching me again, ever.

"What happened to your eye?" she asked.

"I got in a fight in school yesterday."

She signed some papers and we left. At home I looked in the garage and found an old fishing knife. I sharpened it in the woodworking shop at school and from then on I carried it in my pocket. No dude was ever, ever going to do that to me again.

After that night it seemed the least little thing started me fighting. On the school track field one day I got into an argument with this big, stupid Okie named Duke. He started shoving and I shoved back and the next thing I knew we were swinging at each other, kicking, even biting. Mr. Stevenson, the wrestling coach, came over to break it up. He grabbed me and, as he did, Duke hit me in the nose. I was tugging and squirming, trying to get loose. Finally I relaxed a minute and Mr. Stevenson let me go. I whirled around and punched him in the jaw. "You shouldn't have held me while he hit me!" I shouted.

Meanwhile someone had run for Daddy. When he saw me yelling at Mr. Stevenson, he walked over to me and said, "Sammy, shut up."

I did, but it was too late. I had hit a teacher and would probably be suspended. "I'll be by your mama's house this evening to hear your side of it." Daddy said.

I didn't have any side—and I sure didn't want to talk to Daddy. "What time will you be over, Daddy?"

"At six."

"Six o'clock?" I double-checked. That afternoon at 5:30 there was a parents' meeting at the local youth center. Mama and John were going, and I made up my mind right then I was going with them. They didn't know Daddy was coming by the house to talk to me.

They knew nothing about the fight at school.

Since I was going to be suspended anyway, that night at the youth center I decided to stop sneaking off when I wanted a cigarette. Up to this point, I had smoked in only two places, the restroom at school and my bedroom. I lit up and was puffing away when a friend poked me in the ribs. Without saying a word, he pointed toward the entrance. I glanced over . . . and there stood Daddy.

"Sammy, come here."

My first reaction was to stand there. But I knew better. I walked over to him.

"How come you didn't wait at your mother's like I asked you to do? And what's that in your hand?"

"It's a cigarette. Why?" The next thing I knew, Mama and John were picking me up from the floor where Daddy had backhanded me. Mama jumped in front of Daddy, yelling and calling him names. John moved her to the side and told Daddy to hit *him* the way Daddy had hit me.

The police who patrolled the center regularly had gotten out of their car and were standing in the doorway. Daddy and John stood staring at each other, three feet apart.

"John?"

"What, Edward?"

"I want you to know one thing."

"What's that?"

"I'm not afraid of you."

"Sucker, I ain't afraid of you, either."

The police took a step closer. Then the tension broke as Daddy spoke to me.

"Sammy?"

"Huh?"

"Look at me. Your brothers and sisters are at home. Here I am about to get into trouble over you. What will happen if John and I get into a fight and I go to jail?"

"I dunno."

"Well, it's not going to happen. I love you, Sammy. You have no idea how much. I'm going home now. You can come with me if you choose to. Your brothers, sisters and I will welcome you back without any questions. And you know the rules. They haven't changed."

He was waiting for me to make my decision. I couldn't understand why he was doing this. Couldn't he see that I didn't want to be bothered with him anymore?

Yet deep within I wanted nothing so much as to go with him. I wanted to tell my mother, "Mama, I love you, but I'm never going to turn my life around while I live at your house." But the words wouldn't come. Why was there always this battle inside me? One part of me wanted to do right things. The other kept saying, *It's your life. Do your own thing. Enjoy yourself.*

I looked up at Daddy. "Thanks, Daddy, but I'm going with Mama."

"Okay, Sammy," and he walked out.

After that night, I started using more dope. I drank more alcohol, I had more sex. None of it was any good. I was tired of dope, tired of booze, tired of sex—tired of life at 15-and-a-half.

Because of Daddy and Daddy Bryce I was given a second chance at school, but I seldom attended classes. Some days I never got out of my pajamas. I started to think about dying. I talked about dying, even dreamed I was dead. The thought of hell was the only thing that scared me, if it really existed. After a while, even that didn't bother me. Death seemed to be the only way out of my confusion. One night when Mama and John were out I went to the medicine cabinet, emptied all the pill bottles into my pocket and returned to my room. To make sure, instead of water I took a can of lighter fluid and used it to wash down the pills. Boy, did it taste awful—worse than castor oil. I almost threw up after each swallow. After I had taken the last pill, I lay down on my bed. Pretty soon I would know for sure about hell.

The room started to whirl. *Not long now,* I thought. I thought about the group of guys I ran with. *They won't miss me at all.* They were in the same dope/sex/alcohol trap I was in. I said good-bye to my room, shut my eyes. All of a sudden, the lighter fluid started coming back up my throat. I jumped off the bed and stuck my head out the window. I vomited and vomited. When my stomach was empty I still vomited. At last I returned to my bed, thinking, *Not even death wants me.*

I wasn't going to classes that often, but when my brother Buddy was playing I went to the high school basketball games. Buddy could really play basketball. One night he did his normal thing and scored 20 points but our school still lost. My younger brother Tony and I watched together.

After the game Tony walked up to the center on the other team and stuck out his hand.

"I don't shake hands with niggers."

Tony stared at him. "Hey, man," Tony said, "I only wanted to say, 'Great game.'"

"Go to hell, nigger."

That was too much for me. "I don't think I heard clearly what you said," I told the guy. "My little brother only said good game. That racial stuff ain't necessary."

"Get out of my face. You're gonna die, you black nigger. I don't know when or where, but you're gonna die."

My friends were standing there hearing this. The dude was six inches taller than me, but I knew I had to fight. I took my ring off and put it into my pocket. And as I did I felt the knife. *Yeah, I ought to cut this honky!* I cupped the knife in my palm, swung at him and missed. I didn't know how to use a knife in a fight—I had never had it out of my pocket for a fight till this moment.

The dude swung back. I swung again, cutting him above his eye. "Look out!" someone yelled. "He's got a knife!" The dude took off as though the fiends of hell were after him. I chased him for a ways, but I was pigeon-toed—and the guy had legs like stilts.

I was arrested and taken back to Juvenile Hall in Merced. Back to the hall. All the way in the police car my terror rose. Would Chunky still be there? At least I had gained a few pounds and done a lot more fighting. I vowed if I was put into his cell again it would be different.

This time the charge against me was assault with a deadly weapon. I went through the same procedure: took off my clothes, put on the overalls and was marched down the corridor to a cell. To my speechless relief it was empty.

Next morning I was handcuffed and taken to the courthouse. I walked down a long, waxed hall, escorted by a probation officer, to a judge's chambers. Mama and Dad were there. Daddy was there, too. There was a short hearing after which I was taken back to the hall "pending more investigation."

Not knowing how long I would be in there and wanting to get out of my cell as often as possible. I started going to Monday night Bible study. After I completed the third one I was awarded a Bible, a leatherbound Scofield edition. On the inside they wrote, "Presented to Sam Huddleston by Rock Bottom Evangelistic Association." I started looking through it when I got back to my cell. *Hey, this*

ain't no real Bible; there's no words in red. But I kept it.
The next day was Daddy's birthday and I could give it to
him when I got out.

Thirty-seven days later I was released on probation.
The judge said I had been provoked by the racial slurs the
guy made. I was suspended from all schools in Merced
County, except Continuation. I went there only one day.
There didn't seem to be any rules. People were smoking,
cussing the teachers, wandering out of the classrooms
at will. When I got home I told Mama I wasn't going
back. "Why?" "'Cause I'm not stupid; I just make stupid
choices. Besides I'm no dummy."

Mama called a friend of hers named Liz who lived in La
Puente, way down near L.A. She told Mama I could stay
with her and go to Nogales High with her sons.

The day I left I went by Daddy's to give him the Bible.
"Happy belated birthday. Here's a present."

Daddy opened the box. "Oh boy, Sammy, it's a Bible!
It's a nice one! I'm going to save it."

"Save it for what?"

"For you."

"For me?"

"Yes, Sammy. One day you're going to preach out of
this very Bible."

Daddy sure had some crazy ideas.

Mama and Dad drove me to La Puente. They had to leave the next day. Dad had a new job at Castle Air Force Base as a meat cutter and they were moving to Atwater, which was closer to the base. I think Mama felt Liz could handle me because she was a roller derby queen. She stood over six feet and had muscles like a man's.

Nogales High was a huge place. I was amazed at the number of blacks. In the school up north, there were only 10 of us. I never knew there were so many blacks in the whole world. In the lunch area they had Coke, candy and sandwich machines besides the hot lunch line. *Man, this is all right. Now all I need to know is, who's got the dope?* It didn't take me long to find him.

One morning early, Liz woke me up.

"Sammy, Sammy, telephone!"

"Who is it?"

"Go see."

I climbed out of bed and went to the phone. "Hello?"

"Happy birthday to you, happy birthday to you, happy birthday, dear Sammy. . . ." My sisters and brothers were calling to sing happy birthday to me! I had forgotten all about my 16th birthday.

"Hello, Sammy. How does it feel to be 16?"

"Hi, Daddy."

"We just wanted to call you and let you know that we love you, miss you and wish you were home."

"Thanks, Daddy."

I hung up the phone, ran into the bathroom, turned on some water and cried. *Why doesn't Daddy leave me alone?*

That evening Mama and Dad called to wish me a happy birthday. I told Mama I wanted to move back with them. Since they had moved to Atwater, maybe I could enroll in school there. What I really wanted was to be closer to my brothers and sisters. I had thought they hated me, and now I knew they didn't.

A week later Mama called back and said that she and Dad would be there on Friday to pick me up.

Was I ever glad when Friday came. I wanted to get back home. I had been gone for only three months, but it seemed like a year. I had really become a doper. I stayed high as much as possible. It was only when I was high that life was livable.

Before returning to Atwater we stopped in Los Angeles to visit some relatives. They held a party for us. I started drinking, got drunk and passed out. The next morning I started drinking again. I grabbed the first bottle I saw and poured it straight, no mix. I didn't drink for pleasure, only to get drunk.

I went outside and stood by the car. Dad and Mama came down with the suitcases, and the next thing I knew

Dad and I were arguing. We picked it up where we had left off three months before. I cursed him and he cursed me. Mama got between us, her back to me, facing Dad. I threw a punch, connecting with Dad's jaw. He swung at me, but I ducked behind Mama. All the while Mama was yelling, "John, don't you hit my baby. John, you'll hurt him!"

I swung again, ducked again. John picked Mama up, moved her to one side, and before I could run, hit me square in the nose. I rolled over the hood of the car, breaking the antenna, and took off running. A fool I wasn't.

Mama was chasing me, crying and yelling, "Mike, come back!" I ran crying and looking for something to fight with. I soon found an empty beer bottle. I broke it on the street and ran back to where my stepfather was.

"Come on, John, you want to fight?"

"Put that glass down, Mike."

"No way, man, I'm going to cut your throat wide open." I was taking wild swings at him, each time getting closer to his face.

I swung again. This time John struck the bottle out of my hand and knocked me unconscious. I woke up back in the house, in bed, crying, "I'll kill him! I'm going to kill John!'"

Mama and a lot of others tried to calm me down but I kept raving. It must have been painful for Mama to admit she couldn't handle me, but next thing I knew she had telephoned Daddy.

"Sammy, do you hear me?" came his voice over the phone.

"Yes, sir, I hear you."

"Your mama said that you're acting up. You know better, son."

"But Daddy . . ."

"But nothing. You know how to behave, *Sammy*."

"Yes, sir."

"Look, do you want me to come get you?"

He makes it sound like I'm right around the corner, I thought, *when I'm more than 300 miles away.* "That's okay, Daddy. I'm okay now."

"Are you sure?"

"Yes, sir. I'm okay now."

"Okay, I love you. If you change your mind, you call and I'll come."

How many times in the next year I was to wish I had called him back!

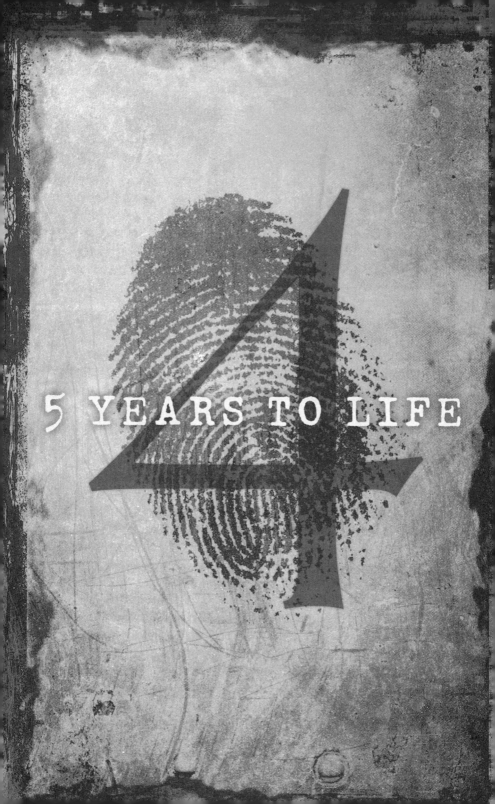

5 YEARS TO LIFE

WHAT IS LIFE?
WHAT DID YOU SAY?
I CAN'T HEAR YOU
PLEASE SPEAK LOUDER

I enrolled at Atwater High School in January 1969, the middle of my sophomore year. I was excited about the change. Maybe I could go straight. Maybe I could stay out of trouble. The school was larger than the one serving Livingston and Delhi, but smaller than Nogales, with fewer blacks and no food machines in the lunch area.

I soon found the partying crowd and began hanging out with them. Hard as I tried not to, it wasn't long before I was back smoking dope, popping pills and boozing it. What started out as a good year was turning sour fast.

Ann and I continued to see each other. I would get a friend's car or steal Mama's car late at night and drive to Delhi. One day I got a call from Ann.

"I've got something to tell you."

"Can you hold on a minute? I'm trying to light a cigarette. Okay, shoot."

"I'm pregnant."

"You're . . . is it mine?"

"Sure it is; you know that."

"I don't know nothing."

"Sammy! You know it's your child. You're the only guy I've ever been with."

"Hey, baby, unless he has a big head and bowed legs, I ain't sure of nothing." I hung up the phone.

Two days later I returned home to find Mama agitated.

"Did you see Ann's father?"

"No, why?"

"He's looking for you. He says he's gonna shoot you for getting his daughter pregnant."

"He's crazy."

"All I know is he had a rifle in his car."

For the next few days I watched slow-moving vehicles closely. Eventually Ann told me he had put the gun away, but still I never visited her when her father was home. I kept denying the baby was mine. Inside I knew it was, but I was scared to admit it.

Things at Mama's house were the same as they had been before I went to La Puente. Dad continued to come home from work, get drunk (what he called "getting mellow") and we would get into an argument or fight, unless it was Saturday. Saturday was the best day of the week. We got up in the morning before dawn. Mama would have packed a big lunch the night before—sandwiches, fried chicken, roast beef. Into the ice chest went beer and sodas. We hitched the boat to the car and set off to the dam.

It took about two hours to get there. I enjoyed watching the sun come up. Everything seemed so peaceful and clean, with big oak trees lining the sides of the road. Most of the time we never paid the entrance fee. We arrived so early and left so late that no one was at the entrance booth to collect.

While Dad backed the boat into the water I held onto the rope, wading into the cold lake in my old tennis shoes. Then all the fishing poles. Worms and tackle boxes went into the boat and away we'd go.

I never could believe all the fish we caught. Perch, catfish, bass, bluegill—once in a while we even caught a trout.

Saturday nights when we got home, if I had a party to go to, Dad excused me from cleaning those stinky fish. I loved catching them, but hated the messy gutting and scraping. Dad was so patient, anything to do with fishing. Maybe it was because fish didn't talk back the way I did.

Though I no longer lived in Livingston, or even went to the same school they did, my sisters, Cynthia and Rhona, were always calling me on the phone, asking me to go to church with them. Finally in a weak moment I told them I would go "some night" to a revival they were all keyed up about.

One Saturday night after Dad and I got the boat back into the garage three friends picked me up to go to a party. Halfway there I remembered that this was the last night of the revival.

"You guys mind if we drop into a church service? We don't have to stay long."

"Why not? Should be good for laughs."

We'd been smoking dope in the car; when we got to the church, we were stoned. When they saw me walk in, my sisters started grinning from ear to ear. They motioned me to sit by them but no way was I going to sit so far up front.

As the four of us slid into the last pew the preacher was talking about how every life needs a touch from God.

"We need a touch from the Lord, all right," one of my buddies whispered, "'cause we sure don't have any money."

After that, each time the preacher mentioned God's touch, we laughed. I don't mean giggle; I mean laugh. We laughed so hard we were rolling on the pew.

"Young men," the preacher said, "you four wearing black leather jackets, you can leave with pure hearts if you surrender your lives to Jesus. He wants to forgive you of your sins and give you a new life." The preacher looked so funny standing there with his arms stretched out that my sides ached from laughing. "Let's get out of here," I said. Maybe without the dope it wouldn't seem so funny.

We went on to the party. As I walked in, someone ran up to me. "Hey, Sammy, your mother's been calling here for you!"

I dialed home.

"Mike," Mom said. "Ann's gone to the hospital. Her labor started this afternoon."

I grabbed my buddy Wayne who had some wheels and we headed for the hospital. We stopped by a liquor store where I bought booze when the owner was drunk enough not to ask for proof of age. He was drunk.

"Give me a six-pack of beer and a pint of peppermint schnapps."

I drank half of it en route. The visitors' door at the hospital opened automatically. I was glad. I wasn't sure I could have found the handle. I had no idea where to go. I stood there looking down the hall.

"Where do people go to have a baby?" I asked a lady sitting at a desk.

"You're looking for the maternity ward," she told me, pointing the way.

I found Ann's room but the nurse wouldn't let me go in. Ann's mother came out.

"You're drunk."

"Naw, I only had a few beers."

"Would you like to see Ann?"

"Is . . . is your husband in there?"

She shook her head. "He just left."

"I'll come in."

Ann was moaning, clutching the sheets. When she saw me she started cursing. "This is your fault! You did this to me! I ought to shoot you myself." I knew when I wasn't wanted and left.

I got out in a hurry. Her mama followed me. "She didn't mean it, Sammy. It's just that having a baby hurts."

I went out to the waiting room. Eventually I must have fallen asleep because I was awakened by a man shaking my shoulder.

"Mr. Huddleston, I'm Dr. Prime. Congratulations! You have a healthy nine-pound-eight-ounce son. He and his mother are both fine."

I pumped his hand up and down, thanking him. Then I sat there. *A son. I've got a son. I'm 16 and I'm a father.*

I jumped up and ran looking for the baby. A nurse pointed out where the newborns were. I beat on the glass, asking which one was mine.

"What's your name, sir?"

"Huddleston. Sam Huddleston."

"There's no Huddleston here."

"There has to be. The doctor said I had a son."

"What's the mother's name?"

"Ann. Ann Ward."

"Here he is. Andre Ward." She held him up. I looked at his tiny hands. His face was wrinkled like a prune. His feet were so small. He had a big head and his legs were bowed.

"Hey, man! That's my kid," I yelled at an orderly passing by.

"Hey, change his last name," I shouted to the nurse through the glass.

"I can't do that."

"Yes, you can. Change his last name to Huddleston. That's my son."

"I'd have to ask the mother."

"Then ask."

The nurse came back, scratched out Ward and put Huddleston. I stood there smiling, thinking, *My own son.* I called Mama and told her she was a grandmother.

I went over to see Ann and the baby the day they came home—making sure first her dad was at work. Ann let me hold Andre. I was scared. His face was red and he had soft fuzz all over his body and a soft spot on the top of his head. When I kissed him he smelled fresh and clean. My son.

"Ann, I'm going to change. I want Andre to have a real father. I'm going to make him proud of me."

For a while I made a real effort to be a different person. But my life was too messed up. I tried to quit smoking but ended up digging in the trash looking for the smokes I had thrown away. I tried to stay out of trouble. I couldn't. I even started to sell drugs to support my own habit. I was in and out of the hall. One day Daddy Bryce came to see me at Mama's. He wouldn't come into the house. He called me out of doors.

"Grandson, I've been hearing bad things about you lately. Folks say you're selling drugs and stealing. I've worked hard to make the Huddleston name one to be proud of. Don't destroy it. Keep in mind, you're a Huddleston, never forget it. So either change your name or your character."

His visit seemed to have the opposite effect of what he intended. I started pestering Mama to get my last name changed. I knew I'd never live up to the one I'd been born with. I went back to Juvenile Hall for burglary this time and was placed on probation. I was really getting hooked on drugs. I couldn't get to sleep without downers; then I needed uppers to get going in the morning. I started keeping a bottle of apple wine in the refrigerator.

I woke up Christmas Day thinking about past

Christmases with my brothers and sisters. I recalled the year Daddy bought me my secret agent cap gun. That was my best Christmas. I loaded it with caps and went around making this big loud bang. I was jerked into the present by the sound of people laughing and popping beer tops in the next room. I looked at my watch. It was past noon. I got up and went to my cousin Shep's house two doors away and started drinking. I didn't want to be in Mama's house. All afternoon I drank at Shep's. Then I decided to go driving. I had bought an old car a week earlier. Mama let me buy it so I could work on it in auto shop at school.

As I started to get into it, Mama came outside. "What are you doing, Mike?" she asked.

"I'm fixing to drive my car."

"You can't drive, you're too drunk." She tried to snatch the keys out of my hand.

I pushed her away. "Mind your own business!"

At that moment my brother Buddy drove up with some gifts for Mama. "Hey, Sammy, don't talk to Mama like that."

"You mind your own business, too!" I took a swing at him. I was so drunk I almost fell.

Buddy grabbed me and put a wrestling hold on me. "Cool it, Sammy." He let me go but not before taking my keys.

After Buddy left, I walked over to Mama demanding the

keys. "Give me my keys. Now."

"Mike! I'm your mother."

At that, something inside me exploded. "You're my what?" I yelled. "I don't need you! I'm 16 and I can make it on my own. When I needed you, when my sisters needed you, where were you then? You were in L.A., too busy to be bothered with us. Mama Carrie is my mama. For all I care, the next time I see you I hope you're in a box."

Mama ran off sobbing to the neighbors'. I followed, shouting through the locked door at her. I had held this thing in for too long, and now it was out. I knew I couldn't live with Mama any longer. Christmas 1970. I went back to Mama's house and called Daddy.

5 YEARS TO LIFE

I ONLY WANTED FUN
NOW SOMEONE'S DEAD
THE CULPRIT?
OH, NO, NOT ME

"God bless you, Huddlestons' residence." At the sound of Daddy's voice on the phone I burst into tears. The booze was kicking my butt.

"What's wrong, Sammy?"

"I want to come home."

"What did you say?"

"I said that I'm tired and I want to come home. Will you come and get me?"

"Where are you?"

"I'm at Mama's."

"I'll be right there." Within 10 minutes Daddy pulled up. I was sitting on a rail in front of the house. He brought the truck to a screeching halt, jumped out and threw his arms around me. It didn't seem to bother him that I was drunk. He and Buddy got my belongings out of Mama's house. She was still at the neighbors'.

The next day, Daddy told me what I had said to Mama.
He had talked to her on the phone. He was ashamed of
me, but not half as ashamed as I felt.

Readjustment at Daddy's house was no small task. I was
used to staying out late, coming home high on drugs or
alcohol. All of that had to change. But it was so great to
be back with them all—Buddy, Tony, Murphy, Cynthia,
Rhona, Daddy and Doll—that I was ready to do anything
to make it work.

I transferred back to Livingston High.

The basketball coach let me join the school team with
the season half over. I think it was because of Buddy. The
coach probably figured that since I was his brother, I'd be
a good ballplayer, too. How wrong can you be!

I started back working with Daddy again. His gardening
business had grown during the three years I had been
gone. It was fun, earning money for a change. I joined
Future Farmers of America again and heard about a
pregnant sow for sale. Daddy and I took a drive out to see
it. The farmer was asking $65. Daddy said it was a fair
price. He said that if the sow had only six piglets I would
make my money back and still have the mother. Since this
would be her second litter, chances were she'd have more
than six.

We bought the animal. Daddy paid half, and we were
partners. We were father and son again. I would wash my
pig, feed her, often just sit on the old wooden fence and
stare at her.

One morning when I was pouring grain into her trough I noticed these little red fuzzy balls nuzzling her. I counted one, two, three . . . 10 piglets! "Daddy," I yelled as I ran toward the house. He walked back with me to see for himself. We stood at the fence looking into the pen. I think what I appreciated most was, Daddy never asked about those years I was away. He talked only about the present and the future. With the 10 pigs the future was looking good.

What I didn't know—what I failed to take into account when I made my high resolves—was that drug use had made me an addict. Without ever intending to, I found myself sneaking off to smoke pot and cigarettes. Many times late at night I climbed out the window—not so easy now that I was sharing a bedroom again—to get the booze I had stolen earlier in the day and hidden in the pigpen. It seemed the harder I tried to quit these habits, the more I would do them. Boy, did I regret ever starting on that stuff! I didn't control my "free" lifestyle anymore; it controlled me.

At last the secrecy, the lying, the continual play-acting in front of those I loved most, became too much for me. I called Mama and asked if I could come back and live with her and Dad again. She sounded reluctant—I knew she was remembering the savage words I'd flung at her on Christmas Day, the last time we'd spoken—but in the end she said yes.

Now I had to tell Daddy and the others. As we came through the front door after church on Sunday evening I plunged in. "Say, uh, I've got, uh, something to say."

They all turned to look at me.

"I'm leaving," I blurted out. "I'm going back to live with Mama."

Rhona and Cynthia stared at me a moment, then started to cry. My brothers also cried, Tony the most. They all began begging me to stay, but I stood there just as Mama had a few years earlier and refused to change my mind. Daddy stepped in front of me. "Sammy, you're 17 now and I can't forbid you to leave. But look at your brothers and sisters. Do you love them?"

"Yes, sir."

"Then how can you hurt them again?"

"I don't know. All I know is that I've got to leave."

"Sammy, how much money did you earn when you lived with your mother?"

"None."

"Now you've got your half of the sow and money in the bank from selling the baby pigs. You can buy your own truck pretty soon. And you say you aren't doing well with us?"

"You don't understand, Daddy." For sure *I* didn't understand why I seemed unable to stop hurting others, hurting myself. To the sound of my sisters' sobs, I packed my suitcase.

The first thing I did at Mama's was apologize to her for the things I'd said on Christmas. I found out that some of my friends in Atwater had started using a hallucinogen called L.S.D. I began using L.S.D. with them. When that wasn't available, I took mescaline, getting so loaded with stimulants I couldn't sleep. I started staying up all night, playing cards and drinking at Shep's house. Shep was six years older than I, but a lot smaller. Maybe because of his size he was always getting into fights. Someone would call the cops and when they came he'd try to fight *them*. It always ended with Shep going to jail with a few lumps on his head.

Daddy came by Shep's house one day looking for me. He found us both loaded on drugs. "Sammy, Shep, I want to talk with you boys."

"Yes, Daddy."

"Yes, Uncle Ray." (His nieces and nephews called him by his middle name.)

He stood staring at both of us. His eyes were red, as if he hadn't slept. "I had a dream last night. I didn't want to tell you about it, but I don't dare not to. Both of you were in the dream . . . and I don't know if it was one of you, or someone else. I do know if you boys don't get your lives right with God, within six months you'll either be dead or kill someone."

Well, I thought, *if there is any truth to that dream I'd better have my good times quick*. I started living it up even more.

To get money for drugs, I stole a checkbook and started writing bad checks. I was caught, sentenced to a youth camp up by the Oregon border and placed on house arrest until a bunk opened up in about a week. I didn't want to go to nobody's camp. What if Chunky was there? No way.

I called my friend Wayne when I got home from court. "Hey, man, since I'll be leaving soon, what say let's party until I do?" Wayne came over and we went from one house to the next smoking dope, drinking beer and dropping pills. We did this for six days. We ended up at Shep's where there was a party going on.

After a while, the booze ran low. I said, "I'll go get some more. Who wants to go with me?" Wayne came over and said, "Sammy, you've had enough. You can hardly stand up now! Go to bed and sleep it off. We've been doing this for a week, man."

"Bug off. If you don't want to go, say so. But don't try to stop me."

"Okay, okay, man. But I'm not going."

So I yelled out again, "Who wants to go?"

"I'll go," said Shep. "If they make you show an ID they'll find out what a kid you are." Shep was always reminding me that big didn't mean much.

"Hey, you guys are too loaded to drive. I'll take you in my car."

"Thanks, Chip."

We were at the liquor store before we realized we hadn't brought cash with us. "Hell, let's hold up the place—scare the dude," I said.

"How you going to scare him?"

"I have a knife," I said.

Shep took the knife. Chip waited in the car, motor running. High as we were, it seemed like the simplest thing in the world.

The store building was divided in half, bar on one side, liquor store on the other with a door connecting the two and one guy running them both. If the guy was in the bar, there'd be no problem.

Shep and I went inside.

"Good evening, may I help you?" The guy was standing behind the cash register.

"Couple bottles of rum and four six-packs of beer."

As he turned to get the beer from the refrigerator, Shep drew out the knife. Suddenly it didn't seem simple. It seemed impossible, crazy. "Let's get the hell out of here!" I whispered. I grabbed a couple of bottles from the shelf nearest me—didn't even know what kind of booze it was—and headed for the door.

I had my hand on the knob when a bottle flew past my head and smashed against the door frame, spraying me with glass. *Don't turn around! Keep going!* But how could

I walk out on Shep? I looked back. Shep was stabbing at the guy, shouting, "Snakes! Snakes!"

The owner was yelling, "Don't stab me anymore, don't stab me anymore!"

I dropped the bottles, ran back and grabbed Shep. "Cool it, man! Cool it!"

"Snakes, Sam! Snakes all over!"

Blood was what was all over. I dragged Shep out the door and we dove into the car. "Come on, man! Punch this thing to the floor."

At Shep's house the party was winding down. I took the knife back—I didn't want Shep flipping out again, hurting someone. Six days of booze and pills were finally getting to me. When a chick said, "Want to go in the bedroom, Sammy?" I said, "Sure."

I needed sleep. Only they wouldn't let me sleep. Someone kept banging on the front door. I yelled out from the bedroom, "Answer the stupid door!" I heard the door open. Then a lot of voices . . . Shep . . . Officer Hank.

It was hours later, at the police station, that I began to remember the liquor store. After that everything was like a nightmare when you can't wake up. The transfer to the adult jail in Merced, the windowless cell with the bed bolted to the wall.

The "visitors' tank" had a plate of glass down the center, with telephones on both sides to talk into. Visiting

day was Friday. Mama came that first Friday. She told me
she had brought me some books and magazines; things
for prisoners had to be left with the guards for inspection
before we could have them. It was strange, talking to
her on the phone when she was two feet away. Our 30
minutes went by fast and I was taken back to my cell. I lay
on my bunk wondering, *Will Daddy come today? Will he
ever come?*

I thought about his dream, and how he tried to warn
me and Shep. How he had pleaded with me time after
time to straighten up. How he had let me come home,
no questions asked—and how I had rewarded him by
walking out again. I thought, *Is this the straw that finally
does it? Has Daddy given up on me?*

Down the block the guard kept yelling the names of
those with visitors. Since Mama's visit this morning, no
Huddleston.

*He's not coming. I don't blame him. What would I do if
someone kept rejecting me the way I rejected Daddy? No
wonder . . .*

"Huddleston, you've got another visitor."

I jumped up and stood in front of my cell door waiting
for the guard to unlock it. *I wonder if it's . . . naw, it's not
Daddy. It's someone else. Daddy's given up on me.*

The guard led the way back to the visiting tank. It was
Daddy. Doll was with him.

I picked up a phone. "Hello, Daddy." I looked down. I couldn't look at his face.

"Sammy," came his voice through the receiver, "we're in trouble and I don't know what we're gonna do. But we're gonna make it. I have no idea what the outcome will be. We're just praying and trusting that Jesus will work it out for your best."

He said a lot more, but I kept hearing those first words: "*We're* in trouble. *We*. Daddy and I. The family and I. Not Sam alone, no matter how many times I'd turned my back on everything Daddy stood for. I hoped I wasn't going to cry; there were other prisoners in the tank.

Daddy passed the phone to Doll. "Hello, sweetie."

"Hello, Doll, how you doing?"

She smiled, showing the gap between her teeth. "We're praying for you. Your daddy brought your Bible."

"What Bible? I don't have a Bible."

"The one you got in Juvenile Hall."

I'd forgotten about it. After a while Doll gave the phone back to Daddy.

"Well, son, our time is about up. Don't forget what I've always taught you. When you're in a place where you need help and I can't be there, call out to Jesus. He will always be there to help."

He's never helped yet, I thought. But I didn't say it.
Daddy was still calling me "son"; that was what mattered.

Tuesday morning, June 14, I appeared in court, where
my case was detained until June 28. On that day I was
detained again until July 2. On July 6 a trial date was set
for August 10. Word from the district attorney's office
was that if I pled guilty the charge would be reduced from
first-degree to second-degree murder/robbery. My public
defender urged me to take it and avoid a trial, so in the
end that's what I did.

Shep chose to go to trial and argue his own defense.
How could I know as I stood beside Shep at the final
hearing that it was the last I'd ever see him? When he had
served ten years of his life sentence he fell ill of a disease
that was never precisely diagnosed. He died in the prison
hospital, not quite 35 years old.

I went to court one more time for sentencing. The judge
pronounced, "Samuel Michael Huddleston, I sentence you
to the state prison at Vacaville for no less than five years
and no longer than the rest of your life." The gavel in his
hand came down with a crack on the table.

I stood there, chains on my ankles, my feet seemingly
welded to the floor. My mother and my sisters ran from
the courtroom crying. "Five years to life" echoed over
and over in my ears. At 17, five years might as well be life.
That night in jail, awaiting transportation to Vacaville,
I asked for some clippers and cut off all my hair. I didn't
want them doing it at the prison as I heard they would.

Also that night Daddy Bryce came to see me. I thought sure he had washed his hands of me. I was the first Huddleston ever to be sentenced to prison. As I entered the visiting tank Daddy Bryce was already holding a phone. I picked up the phone on my side of the glass. "Grandson," came his voice from the receiver, "when you get to prison, hold your head high and tell the truth to everyone. Remember, you're still a Huddleston."

I hadn't looked up when I sat down. But when he said, "You're still a Huddleston," I looked at him. He stood there proud in his Stetson hat, tears running down his cheeks. I had never seen my grandfather cry.

Next day I was taken from my cell, my wrists handcuffed in front of me, my ankles chained again. Another chain was wrapped around my waist, connected to my wrists and ankles. I could step only six inches at a time.

I shuffled out to a waiting sheriff's station wagon. Two other guys who were going to prison that day were already in it. As we drove through the streets of Merced, I stared at the buildings and trees trying to imprint them on my memory. We passed the bus station and I thought about the time Sara and I ran away.

Vacaville was over 150 miles north, on past Sacramento. As we pulled onto Route 99 I recalled all the times I had traveled this road in Daddy's truck, driving down to see Daddy Bryce and Mama Susie in Merced, then back home to Livingston. We passed through Atwater and I wondered what my friends were doing. Would any of them miss me?

We came to Livingston. Route 99 went right by our house. I wondered if anyone would be in the yard, waving or something, but there was no one in sight. There was the pen where I had kept my pig. And the bedroom window I used to sneak out of in search of freedom. Now there were chains on me, and any window I'd be looking out of would have bars.

We crossed the Merced River and were in Delhi. Andre lived here with his mother. How old would he be when I returned? When would I see him again? Would he hate me? Would he grow up to be like me? *Oh, God, don't let him be like me.*

As we left Delhi behind I thought of Mama Carrie. I wondered if she would even be alive when I came back home. Would I ever hug her neck again? I had to stop thinking about the family. I had to think about where I was going and how I would survive.

"Hey, officer, got a cigarette?"

"Sure, son." He lit it and passed it back to me through the wire mesh that separated us.

I took a deep, long drag, sat back and started blowing smoke rings. It all still seemed like a nightmare. I didn't know the nightmare hadn't started yet.

My High School Graduation picture
(although I actually completed HS while
in prison at Tracy Adult School)

PRIVILEGE CARD
CALIFORNIA
DEPARTMENT OF CORRECTIONS

B 36718
6 M HUDDLESTON
9   7   71

B-36718
HUDDLESTON, S.M.

Prison picture

Me and the family at Mt. Hermon
in the redwoods

My father and his brothers. They all had a profound impact on me becoming the man I am.

Mama Carrie (my grandmother who helped my father raise us)

Tracy Adult School

Tracy, California

This Certifies That

Samuel Michael Huddleston

Has completed a Course of Studies in accordance with the requirements
of the State Board of Education and the Trustees of this school and is
therefore awarded this

High School Diploma

Given this month of July, nineteen hundred seventy-two

Steven J. Arnaudo
President Board of Trustees

Sheila G. McClellan
Clerk Board of Trustees

James R. French
District Superintendent

Richard L. Froman
Principal

High School Diploma (earned while at Deuel Vocational
Institution, Tracy, CA)

My wedding day

Royce – high school
grad photo

Ericka – high school
grad photo

Andre – high school
grad photo

Terry and Mary Inman, the pastor who gave me a chance to be his youth pastor.

Steve & Brenda Madsen and their boys. My mentor as a youth pastor and dear friend.

Part of my youth group at Church on the Hill

Me, Daddy and President Reagan while
I was Executive Director of M-2

Bill Lyon and me on top of a glacier in Alaska.
We were on a cruise celebrating my 50th birthday. Bill was my VP at M-2 and a dear friend.

Bethany graduation
picture with Linda

Lighthouse Covenant Fellowship staff picture

A few of the men from my pastoring days at
Lighthouse Covenant Fellowship

Me and Glen Morrison, Follow Up Prison Ministry
(we prisoners refer to him as the godfather of
prison ministry)

Azusa Pacific University graduation
picture with Linda

With Rev. Godwin
Ahiljah in Ghana,
West Africa

Me and Linda in Mexico

Me and Linda in Italy

Me and Linda in Belgium

Me and my baby Ericka in Italy after she graduated from UC Berkeley

Venice, me and Linda in Piazza San Marco celebrating our 30th wedding anniversary

Fiji with my spiritual parents, Rev. G. Lee and Sandy Thomas. When I was in prison he visited me.

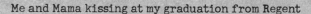

Mama and Dad (more than a step-father)

Me and Mama kissing at my graduation from Regent

My Pastor Bishop Donald Green and wife, Betty, at his 40th celebration of pastoring San Francisco Christian Center

Me and Mama on Alaskan cruise after Dad's death.

Me being prayed over after being elected as the assistant superintendent of the Northern California and Nevada District, Assemblies of God

Me and my granddaughters in Ghana

Me and Linda (after 30 years)

Me in my graduation robe

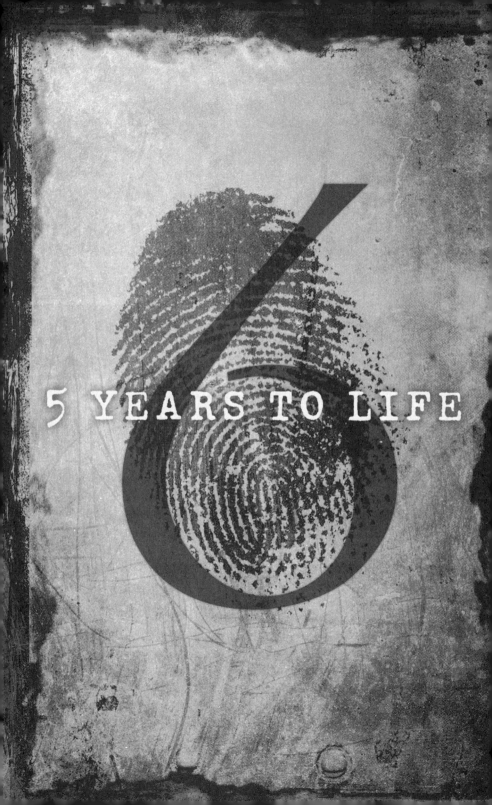

5 YEARS TO LIFE

I'VE BEEN PLACED
IN THIS PRISON
AT THE AGE OF SEVENTEEN
I WONDER IF I'LL
EVER SEE THE OUTSIDE
WORLD AGAIN

"Hey, man, wake up." The prisoner next to me nudged me in the ribs as the wagon arrived in Vacaville. I leaned over—the chains wouldn't let me lift my arms above my chest—and wiped my face with my hands. We had stopped in front of some long, white buildings surrounded by two fences six feet apart topped with razor wire and monitored from gun towers. "Dead man zone," the guy next to me said. "They catch you between those fences, they shoot."

The electric gate in front of us was sliding from left to right. The guard in the tower waved us forward. *Oh, God,* I thought, *this is it.*

We entered and the gate behind us closed. There was another gate in front of us. A guard walked over to the wagon and the driver handed him some papers. The guard looked in, nodded and stepped back. The second gate rolled open.

The car stopped again, this time under an archway. To

our right was a big green steel door. I heard a buzzer and the door opened. We got out one at a time and hobbled through the door like ducks. I jumped as the door slammed shut.

My chains were taken off. The guard who had accompanied us from Merced looked at me. "Good luck, Huddleston, you're going to need it." I watched as the door reopened and closed on my last contact with home.

"All right, you guys, take off those street clothes and head for the showers." Uniformed guards and guys dressed in blue Levis and denim shirts were standing around watching us. My companion from the wagon explained that the guys in blue were convicts, assigned to this reception area.

I took my clothes off slowly. The guys in blue were staring. I jumped into the shower. I noticed the other new arrivals kept their butts to the shower wall. So did I.

We put on prison outfits and carried our own clothes to a long counter. "You can send them home at your own expense or donate them to Goodwill." I glanced at my things. Mama had collected my pants from under the bed at Shep's and brought them to me at the county jail. Though they had been washed they still had faded bloodstains on them.

"Naw, man, I'll donate this stuff."

"Stand over here," said one of the duty prisoners. He put some numbers on a board, stuck them in front of my chest and took a picture.

"This is your number, B-36718, for as long as you are in prison. Don't forget it. How much time you got, anyway?"

"Five years to life."

"You'll be around awhile." I glanced at the date on the receipt I had been given for my clothing. September 7, 1971, the day I became a number.

While I was fingerprinted a guard looked through my papers. "You're only 17? You're too young for Vacaville. We'll have to transfer you to D.V.I."

"What's D.V.I.?"

"Another prison. Down in Tracy. Deuel Vocational Institution. Better known as gladiator school."

I wondered what "gladiator" meant.

Two hours later I was shackled again—wrist, ankles and waist—and shuffled out to a waiting car. Tracy was down south of Vacaville, halfway back to Merced.

"We'll be on the road two hours," the guard who accompanied me said, "so relax." He gave a kind of chuckle. "It'll be the last chance you get to relax."

The guard told me that Tracy was divided into two prisons. One was the processing center for new arrivals. Sometimes inmates stayed there for months. From there you could be sent to any prison in California, including next door to the mainline at D.V.I. "Mainline's mostly young men, early 20s. There's lots of fights, killings, rapes."

I was beginning to grasp the meaning of *gladiator*.

At Tracy we drove up a long driveway with tall trees on each side. The lawn had been freshly cut: the smell reminded me of Livingston. Again we drove through a set of gates set in double fences. I counted six gun towers, just the part I could see.

In reception the chains, shackles and cuffs were taken off. I had to take another shower, another picture, get fingerprinted again. I was given some ragged underwear, a pair of gray socks, brown lace-up boots, bedding, toothbrush, tooth powder, a bar of soap, a small black comb, which I didn't need with my hair all gone, and some tobacco with papers to roll cigarettes. The prison clothes here were green. Finally I was escorted outside to the "cage" between two cell blocks: a sea of green Levis and green shirts. Some of the inmates were playing basketball, others chess, checkers or dominos; some lifted weights, others just walked back and forth. It hit me. *I'm here. I'm really in prison.*

A basketball rolled in front of me. This guy came to get it. He looked at me and started laughing.

"What the hell is so funny?"

He pointed to my head. "Man, you've got a big head. I'm gonna call you 'Headquarters.' " He walked away still laughing.

The cellblocks at Tracy were three tiers high. At count time a guard took me to a cell at the far end of the first tier. On the way we passed a large room filled with round tables and short round stools, all bolted to the floor. The chow hall. The guard opened a wall box and pulled a handle down. There was a clanging of metal and my cell door rolled to the left. I walked in. More clanging as it closed. I stood there. The cell was just like the county jail except it had a window. I was scared and tired after the long day of traveling and going through two entry routines. I flopped onto the bunk and fell asleep.

I awoke the next morning to shouts of "Reveille! Reveille! Reveille!" I rolled out of my bunk and my feet hit the cold concrete floor. I put my feet back onto the bunk, reached over the side, grabbed my socks and put them on. I stood up, took a step and drained my bladder. Over the toilet was a small metal mirror. I hated the face that looked back at me. Baldheaded. Skin pasty from lack of sun ever since June, and pimply from the rotten food in the Merced jail.

I dressed in my green shirt and pants and waited for my cell door to open. At last it clanged aside and I joined the line of men outside the mess hall. Inside the door I picked up a metal tray and inched along the food line. "Hey," I said to the guy ahead of me, "what's that stuff he put in your bowl?"

"Oatmeal."

I didn't know what it was, but oatmeal it wasn't. And I had thought the food in Merced was bad. "I don't eat that crap."

"Listen, take everything they give you. You can always give it away or sell it. How much time you got, anyway?"

"Five to life."

He grinned. "You'll be eating a lot worse garbage than this before you leave."

I stayed in the processing center several weeks before being transferred next door to the mainline. The mainline had a central corridor that connected the entire prison. It looked a mile long. Off to each side were the cell blocks. Each block had a small common room with wooden benches facing a TV mounted on the wall. About halfway down the hall was control. The entire prison was operated from within that small office. Near control were the Catholic and Protestant chapels and further down, the four chow halls. At the end was a huge gym and just before you got to the gym, two iron doors that led to a big yard area. There was a football field, a baseball diamond, a weight pile and a swimming pool that was no longer used. Too many people had mysteriously drowned.

In a separate section were the industry and trade areas. Convicts had to walk through a metal detector when returning to their cells from this area, yet somehow handmade knives, I learned, were always getting in.

I was assigned to the steam line serving vegetables. The first day this black dude came up, held out his tray and told the white guy working next to me to give him a little rice. He gave him a small scoop. "Don't be funny, man, give me more than that." The white guy slammed a second scoop of rice onto the tray. The black dude jumped over the steam table and started stabbing the white dude with a fork. I stood there too stunned even to run. Another black guy jumped over the steam table, pushed me up against the wall, said, "Excuse me, little brother," and started hitting another white dude in the face with his fist. He then jumped back over the table, got in line and stood there as though he had done nothing. Five years of this? This is crazy! This is madness. Whistles were blowing, guards arriving on the run.

I watched, amazed, but soon discovered that similar things happened every day. Tension was always high, fights commonplace.

I hated working in the kitchen. If you gave a guy too much food the guard gave you a CDC-115, which was a negative written report that went into your file. But if you didn't give an inmate enough to suit him, he'd wait for a chance to get you later.

I went before the classification board to request a job change. This board made all decisions about inmates at D.V.I. If you wanted to attend school or learn a trade, they had to approve it first. Eventually they assigned me a job as a clerk, paying $10.50 a month. Each morning after breakfast I had to report back to my cell, clean it, then wait for release to my job. It was nice because I worked on the shipping dock at the back of the prison. Even though I was still inside the cyclone fences, I was outside the cell block.

My main concentration was on staying alive. I was told that if you make it the first 90 days, you'll be all right. "Just remember," one convict told me, "mind your own

business, don't gamble or mess with homosexuals." I
could handle that.

I hated the count before dinner. When the guard yelled
count time, we returned to our cells and were locked in.
Then we had to stand in front of the doors so that when
the guard walked by he could count us without having to
stop.

One day my name was called over the intercom.
"Huddleston, B-36718—that's B-36718—report to
control. You have a visitor." I went to control, got a pass
and was told where the visiting room was. There weren't
many visitors: I figured it was an off day. It didn't take
long to spot my family. There were all my brothers and
sisters plus Daddy and Doll. Cynthia was holding a baby.
Andre!

The room had tables and chairs that could be moved.
In the center of the room was a desk on a tall platform.
The visiting room officer sat up there to keep a watch on
everyone. I gave him my pass and joined my family. We
could only embrace at the beginning and end of a visit,
and we had to keep our hands on the table the whole
time, but it was a thousand times better than having that
glass between us in Merced.

They stayed three hours and it seemed like three
minutes. Returning to the cell block after a visit, though,
was a bummer. You had to be strip searched. "Take off all
your clothes and do what I say," barked the officer. "Open
your mouth, move your tongue around, lift your arms,
open your fingers, move your penis from side to side,
turn around, lift your feet, bend over, spread your cheeks,

cough." This was the routine after every visit to make sure you weren't smuggling in drugs.

November 26. I didn't tell anyone it was my 18th birthday. At mail call some cards were slid under my cell door. They were from Mama and my brothers and sisters, but none from Daddy. I lay on my bunk trying to figure out why Daddy didn't send a card. Suddenly there was a rap on the window of my cell door. I looked out and saw it was someone with a priest's collar. It was the chaplain. "Are you Sam Huddleston?" he asked.

"Yes."

"B-36718?"

"Yes."

"Your father called and asked me to wish you a happy birthday in person and to tell you he loves you and is praying for you."

"Thanks, chaplain, thanks a lot."

One day when I went to the shower there were two other guys in there, Slickster and Cool. "Man, Headquarters, you sho' got some big backs," said Cool.

"I agree with you," piped in Slickster. I had been in prison long enough to know they were talking about my butt. I dried off and put my clothes on. "My cell is J-136," I told them. "You come calling, it could be the last call you ever make." I walked away like I was the toughest dude in the place, but I was shaking so hard I was sure they saw.

Back in my cell I worked at filing the handle of my
toothbrush to a point against the concrete floor. I
didn't want to fight, but this was war and I was the
battleground. I knew if the guards found my "weapon"
I'd be given more time, but it would be better than what
those guys had in mind. I hid the toothbrush inside the
rim of my toilet.

After the shower incident Slickster backed off but Cool
didn't. He razzed me daily. He had others come up and
tell me how bad he was and what he had done to guys.
He challenged me to box in the block without gloves.
I declined and he called me a coward. He entered the
common room one day while I was watching TV and
slapped me on the back of the head. I jumped up. "That's
it, Cool. I've had enough of your tripping. Let's get it on."
The others watched us. They knew this was coming. Two
guys would slug it out until one went down. That one
became the girl of the winner.

Cool threw the first punch, connecting with my midriff.
"Is that your best shot?" I needled him. He threw another
one. "Come on, Cool, I know you can do better than
that." I figured if I got him mad enough he'd get wild and
I could nail him.

The opening came. I hit him with a right to the jaw, a
left in the stomach and a right to the solar plexus, bending
him over, knocking the wind out of him.

I stood totally still as he hung onto my shoulder with his
right hand. If I pushed him, humiliating him further, he or
one of his cronies would kill me. Not now, but when the
opportunity came. I whispered to Cool, "If you mess with

me again I'll kill you." It had all happened so fast that when the guards showed up it was over. We made like it was just a friendly scuffle so we wouldn't get a 115.

On my way to chow one day I had my first run-in with a guard. "Hey, you. Come here." I kept walking. I was getting good at pretending I didn't hear. He grabbed my arm and threw me up against the brick wall. It was a lieutenant.

"Say, what's the problem?"

"No problem. Just shut up, put your hands on the wall and spread your legs."

"For what?"

"Because I said so."

I faced the wall and was patted down. "Okay, wise guy, what are you doing with carpet wrapper around your waist?" I didn't answer. We both knew why. If someone stabbed me it would protect my gut. He peeled it off me. "Get the hell out of here." I couldn't figure out why he stopped me. Had he done so an hour earlier he'd have caught me with the knife I'd smuggled from the shipping dock. It hadn't taken long at D.V.I. to realize that the strong survived and the weak perished.

A couple of days later I was about to enter the chow hall again when whistles started blowing. I braced my back against the wall. A fight had broken out, two Mexicans, both with knives. Guards came running from everywhere. The riot gates were closed and powdered gas was shot, filling the corridor with smoke. A bunch of us covered our faces and ran into the chow hall. The door was slammed and locked. Noticing there were fewer whites than blacks locked in the hall, this big black yelled, "Let's get these suckers." We moved in on them. Someone hit me with a silverware container but I kept swinging. Knives were pulled out and a lot of people were stabbed. The big black guy got stuck three times in the back. Blood was everywhere. We didn't think the white guys had knives, but we were wrong. Soon the fighting spread throughout the entire prison and a major riot was underway. Though I fought as hard as anyone, I was terrified; I'd never been in anything like this before.

I hated guards—whites, Mexicans and blacks. Especially blacks. I was young and really into the black brothers unity thing—until my run-in with Slickster and Cool in the shower. That's when I realized color meant nothing. Though I ran around with a few black guys for protection, I could never let my guard down around them either. The only place to breathe easy was in my locked cell at night.

There, though, I faced another kind of terror. It was nine months now since Shep and I had entered that liquor store—time, I thought, for the horror of that scene to begin to fade. Instead, the opposite was happening. Details of that night, which at first I'd had trouble recalling at all, were growing sharper, nearer, until when I was alone I could think of nothing else. Night after night I'd be jerked out of sleep by a voice pleading, "Don't stab me! Don't stab me anymore!" I began fighting sleep to silence those cries.

Murders were commonplace at D.V.I. When the count

was extra long the whispers would travel along the tiers of locked cells. "Who's missing?"

"Indian."

"Thrown off the upper walkway."

Keeping busy was my handhold on sanity. I had a semester of high school left to finish; I enrolled in the adult school. I went to school in the morning, to my job in the afternoon and worked out in the gym at night, lifting weights to develop muscles that might ward off the predators.

At the gym I also learned to box. A guy named Twin trained me. He told me he had once fought for Archie Moore and that Archie had visited him at D.V.I., his only visit in seven years. By now I knew that that empty visiting room, on my family's regular trips to see me, was not a fluke: Most inmates got no visits.

Within six months I had finished school and received my high school diploma. It said "Tracy Adult School" and didn't have D.V.I. or prison on it. I was proud. I mailed it home to Mama.

On Sundays, in the beginning, I went to the Protestant church service. Most of the other blacks who were religious attended the Muslim service held in the library farther down the corridor. When I made that left into the Protestant chapel, I was called every name in the book.

"Oh, nigger, leave that white man's religion alone."

"Haven't you been held down enough? Come on with us, brother, and be set free."

Finally I gave in to the pressure and started attending the Muslim services. The imam would open his sermon, "Brothers, we are oppressed. We've been oppressed for centuries. You are behind bars because of your oppressors and we all know who that is, the white man."

"Amen!" would come the response from the audience.

There was never a white face in sight. Even the guards who stepped in to check things out were black. Encouraged by the brothers, I started reading the Holy Koran. Since I didn't read well, I read slowly. I really liked the ideas in it and the things the imam told us. I tried them on my family when they came to visit.

"Mama Carrie, how come you press your hair with a hot comb?"

"What, baby?"

"How come you and Mama press your hair straight?"

"It looks good."

"That's not the reason. It's because you want to be white."

"What's wrong with you, boy?"

"The church has fooled us. The true religion is Islam. Black people who go to church are still slaves to the white man. Not me. I reject the white man's God. It's His fault I'm here."

Mama Carrie's eyes got wide. "I'll be praying for you, baby."

I joined any program that would fill the hours. I enrolled in a class called creative dynamics. The instructor taught us to think positive thoughts about ourselves. The course lasted 16 weeks and I really enjoyed it. I lay in my cell at night and told myself, "You're not a bum; you really are special. You can do great things." It didn't work. As soon as the course ended, I was thinking negatively again. How could I kid myself about my life when I was 18 years old and in prison for murder? I was no good, and I knew it. All the positive thinking in the world couldn't change that, or stop the cries of the store owner from waking me at night.

For all the vigilance of the prison authorities, drugs were easy to get at D.V.I. I knew they were messing me up, so I joined Narcotics Anonymous. Most of the guys admitted they were going through the program only to help them get a release date. I attended a few meetings, then quit in disgust at the phony testimonies. I tried Alcoholics Anonymous and quit that, too. I didn't like standing in front of a roomful of people saying, "Hello, I'm Sam and I'm an alcoholic."

Daddy wrote that Daddy Bryce had cancer and had gone to the hospital. There was a telephone next to his bed, so I applied for permission to make an outside call. I was assigned a time slot on Wednesday.

On Tuesday I heard my name over the intercom. '"Huddleston, B-36718, that's B-36718, report to control."

The young guard behind the small window didn't even look up. I put my face up to the window. "I'm Huddleston."

"What's your number?"

"B-36718."

"Your grandfather is dead."

I just stood there staring at him. "Huddleston, get back to the yard. You've got your message." I kept staring. I wanted to rip his face off. How could Daddy Bryce be dead?

At last I went back to the yard. Daddy Bryce . . . he and my daddy were the only men I had ever respected. I felt like crying but I knew better than to show emotion in front of other prisoners. It would be taken for weakness. I lit up a cigarette and walked around the yard, thinking of how much faith Daddy Bryce had in me and how I'd let him down.

When the yard call was complete I went to see my counselor about placing an emergency phone call. Daddy answered the phone.

"God bless you, Huddlestons' residence."

"They gave me the news, Daddy. When is his funeral?"

"Saturday. Is there any way you can be there, Sammy? Would they allow it?"

"I dunno. Sometimes, if it's your immediate family."

"Who would I have to talk to?"

I put him on the line with my counselor and three days later was granted a T.C.R. (Temporary Community Release) to attend the funeral.

All the way there I gaped out the car window at the color everywhere—in trees, flowers, new-model cars, stores, well-dressed people. When we arrived the church was full. We inched our way through the crowd and I squeezed between two cousins. The guard sat in the rear. Each time I glanced back he was looking at me. There was singing, a eulogy by one of my uncles, more singing, a sermon. Daddy sat beside Mama Susie; both of them were crying. Some women in the congregation screamed, a few fainted, letting out their emotions.

The time came to say good-bye to the body. I approached the coffin slowly and stood, staring down at Daddy Bryce. He had gotten so small from the cancer. His Stetson hat rested on his hands. I remembered how tall he always looked in his sheriff's uniform. I thought about how hard he worked to build a good name for our family, and how I had destroyed it. No one rushed me. I stood there and thought of how he used to pat me on the head and say, "You're a Huddleston, never forget it." I began speaking to him. "I'm going to make you proud of me, Daddy Bryce. I'm going to build our name back up. I don't know how, but I'm going to be the person you believed in." I reached down and stroked the rim of his hat. At the close of the service I had only a moment to speak to Daddy. This was the first time in my life when he needed me, and where was I? Having to go back and be locked up. I couldn't even stand by my own father at a time like this. I looked him in the eye. "Daddy, I'm going to change. I don't know how, but I'm going to change, you'll see. I'm going to make you proud." He patted my shoulder. He had heard it all before. When I moved back home on Christmas, two years before . . . when Andre was born.

This time I made up my mind it was going to be different.

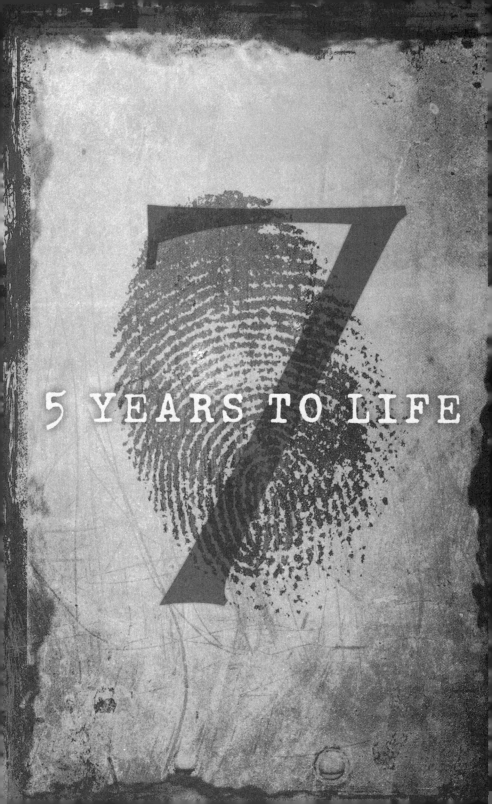

I KNOW THAT I'M IN PRISON DON'T KNOW WHEN I'LL GET OUT BUT MY SOUL HAS BEEN SET FREE AND FOR THAT I'M GOING TO SHOUT

In February 1973 I was called for my first board appearance. The board was the group of individuals who determined when a prisoner was ready for parole, the decision based on time served, severity of crime, and how little trouble you caused while in prison. Though I hadn't caused any trouble—or hadn't been caught—I knew that 18 months wasn't long enough for my crime. Yet I couldn't help hoping.

When the day came I woke up, so anxious that I leaned over the toilet and threw up. I sat in the waiting area afraid I was going to be sick again. When my name was called I forced a smile and entered the boardroom. Two men sat at a table.

"What the hell you smiling for?" one of them snapped. "Maybe you don't know why you are here. Allow me to tell you. You and your cousin killed another human being. I bet you think that's funny?"

"No, sir, I . . ."

"I bet you don't even feel remorse."

"Sir . . ."

"Shut up, B-36718. I know your type."

I clamped my teeth together. I had been told they tried to make you blow it so they could justify denying you.

"You got anything to say?"

"No, sir."

"Then get out of here. By the way, you have been denied parole. You're not ready yet."

I left the room, went to the weight pile in the yard and lifted weights. I didn't talk to anyone; the other inmates seemed to know what I was feeling. When yard call was complete, I went to my cell and stayed in for the rest of the night. I didn't want to risk punching someone out because of how I felt toward that board member.

Two days later I got the official denial in the mail. My next appearance was scheduled for February 1974.

Before that time arrived, however, I requested and was granted a transfer out of D.V.I. and into the forest-fire-fighting program made up of prisoners who volunteered for this service. Those of us making the transfer were dressed in white overalls, chained—wrists, ankles, waist—and loaded onto the prison bus that we called the Gray

Goose. Inside the bus we were allowed to take any seat we chose. Now that was different, being able to make a choice. Normally we were told everything—when to get up and go to bed, when to eat, how much to eat, when to work, when to play. The driver and the two guards on the bus had guns. One guard sat up front with the driver behind a wire fence, the other in a wire cage in the back.

We drove due east, into the mountains. As on the trip to Daddy Bryce's funeral, my eyes couldn't drink in enough of the color everywhere. A sign told us we had arrived: "Sierra Conservation Center." This was headquarters for the statewide forest fire control system manned by inmate volunteers. There were no fences, no razor wire at Sierra, just high concrete walls and fewer gun towers in comparison with the nine at D.V.I. The major difference was, no cells. We lived in dorms, 16 men to each one, and we could stay out on the yard until 9:00 P.M. I hadn't been outside after 3:30 since I came to prison. No long corridors and a lot more openness: baseball fields, horseshoe pits, a handball court.

At chow time that first night, however, I saw some of the white guys I had rioted against at D.V.I. I couldn't sleep that night or for many nights thereafter. I hated those open dorms and realized just how secure my locked cell had been.

Easter morning of 1973 found me at my usual Sunday morning task, lifting weights. I had been working out only 15 minutes when Mark came up.

"Hey, Sammy, what you doing this morning around nine o'clock?"

"Just what I'm doing now."

"How about going to church with me?"

"You know I don't go to church. Church is for whiteys and niggers who want to be slaves to whiteys."

"Come on, Sammy. It's Easter."

"I don't care what day it is. I'm free of all that mumbo-jumbo. It's all lies, anyway."

"You know, Sam, when we were at D.V.I. you dared me to smoke dope with you and I did. How come you won't go to church with me? Are you scared?"

"Scared? Scared of what, man? Leave me alone."

"I won't leave you alone unless you go to church with me."

In the end, to get the guy off my back, I went. Right away I was sorry. As I sat in the pew, I couldn't help but think about Daddy—the kind of father he had been, and the kind of father I had turned out to be. For months I had managed not to think about those things. What kind of memories would Andre have—if he remembered me at all? When the preacher said, "Amen," I almost ran out of the church.

The next week was terrible. All I could think about was Andre, and how I wanted him to be proud of me. I heard the chaplain had a group that met with him once a week. If something was bugging you, you could talk about it.

I joined and I really liked the group. I had never talked the way we did. The chaplain would ask a question, get us going on it and sit there puffing his pipe. He wouldn't give us answers, but he did raise a lot of questions.

I was assigned to the kitchen as a cook's helper. It was great. I could steal sugar, Kool-Aid and other stuff to sell in the dorm. The assistant cook was a nice guy named Jess, a real silent, mean-looking dude. One day when I was washing dishes, though, Jess started talking.

"I had a visitor yesterday," he said.

He must have said it ten or twelve times. He couldn't stop talking about this guy who had come to see him as part of a program called M-2—Match-Two. An individual from outside, Jess explained, was "matched" with an individual prisoner who didn't get many visits. "He's coming back next month," Jess kept saying. "He'll do it. He'll come."

The way Jess talked, I didn't think he had ever had a visit before.

My family didn't get up to Sierra as often as they had to D.V.I. but they still came, and in addition I was allowed to phone home once a week—Thursday nights at 8:30 was my assigned time.

One Thursday evening I was thinking so hard about Andre I almost let the time slip by. *What will it be like when he gets older? When he sees me walking down the street, will he come up to me and call me Dad or will he be ashamed and pretend he doesn't know me? How can I be a father he'll look up to? I can't. It's too late. I'm doing five years to life. Even if I got out tomorrow, I'm marked for the rest of my days.*

What if I change? No dope, no booze, no stealing . . . no way. I've been doing that stuff too long, since those guys gave me that sloe gin when I was 13. If they hadn't talked me into taking a drink, the time we had that tractor show. . . . If David hadn't given me those cigarettes—kept giving them to me till smoking grass was a habit I couldn't quit. . . . I looked down at my watch. Eight-forty! I had almost missed my phone call!

I ran to the front office and dialed my mother's number. It rang and rang. No one home. Ten minutes late and she couldn't wait? My one phone call all week, and she's got something more important. Something else is always more important to Mama. That's how I ended up the way I am: It wasn't David, or the guys at school; it was Mama walking out on us when I was 8 years old.

I'd phone Daddy . . . Daddy always stood by me, and there was always somebody home at his house. No answer at Daddy's either. . . . I held the phone in my hand and listened to it ring. *They've all forgotten me. Probably some big deal at church. . . .* Church always came first with Daddy, no matter how much he claimed he loved his family. It was his everlasting churchgoing that drove Mama away and broke up our home. I was dialing frantically now every number I knew—cousins, friends, friends of friends. All that answered me was the mechanical buzz of the receiver.

My telephone time was up; the next dude was waiting.

I walked out into the yard feeling lonelier than I ever had in my life. I thought about something Daddy used to say. If we ever came to a point in life when we needed a friend and no one was there, God would always be at our side, waiting. "Closer than hands or feet," Daddy used to say.

I flopped down on the grass and looked up at the stars. Where was God? Someone else who was supposed to be there, and wasn't. "I can see my hands and feet," I said out loud, "but I sure can't see You."

I waited a moment, half-hopeful, but I saw nothing, heard nothing. Except my own voice—my voice as I'd never heard it before. *It's their fault. They made me drink. It's George's fault. He snitched on Shep and me. It's Mama's fault. She went away. It's Daddy's fault. It's God's fault.*

And then a voice that was definitely not my own: *Sam, how long are you going to blame others for the choices you make?*

The grass was damp, the wet soaking through my clothes, but I sat there stunned, listening to thoughts in my head that I knew weren't my thoughts. *When are you going to take charge of your life, Sam? I can't help you with your life until it's yours. Not David's. Not your mother's. When are you going to take control of your life?*

"God," I whispered hoarsely, "is this You?" Knowing it was. Knowing these ideas weren't coming from me. "God, if You're really there . . . really here . . . if it's all true, like Daddy says. . . . God, I'm not asking to go home. I'm just asking You to help me change. Now. Here in prison. It's right—what You said—I'm in prison because I fouled up. Me. No one else. Over and over. But God, if You're real, and if You'll help me, I'm going to be different."

I went to my dorm and wrote a letter to Daddy, telling him I'd made the first real prayer of my life. Then I went to bed. I was washing dishes after breakfast next morning when I realized . . . not once in the night had I sat up with the screams of the store owner jerking me awake. For the first time in two years I had slept through the night. Was it really God I had heard, there under the stars? Was He really going to help me?

I was almost afraid to go to bed that night, but again I slept soundly and peacefully. This had to be God. In fact, the more I thought about Thursday night, the more sure I was: What were the chances of everyone I knew being out when I telephoned?

I wanted to tell Mark, but he'd been shipped out to one of the firefighting camps. I started reading my Bible—the one I got in Juvenile Hall and gave to Daddy—and tried to change my behavior.

The first thing I decided to work on was my language. I didn't know how much I cursed until I tried to stop. Also I started praying at bedtime, down on my knees the way Daddy taught us when we were little. If the guys stared, that was their problem.

The next group meeting I stayed afterward and told the chaplain what was happening in my life. He suggested I read some spiritual books so I could, as he put it, grow as a Christian.

When Daddy came to visit that month he almost ran over the guard getting to me. He grabbed me, picked me right up off the floor and almost squeezed the breath out of me as he stood there and cried. "Nineteen years," he kept saying, "19 years, since the day you were born, I been praying."

Daddy sent me a real nice eight-track tape player and some Christian music tapes. I put it on top of my locker and found out my temper was the next thing I had to work at. The guy in the bunk next to mine accidentally knocked the tape player to the floor. I told him I'd smash his face in if it was broken and I couldn't listen to my Christian music.

Also, I kept stealing from the kitchen. One of the guys in the dorm came up to me one day. "Hey, man, I noticed at night you read your Bible."

"Yeah."

"And you kneel beside your bed and pray."

"So what?"

"I mean, that's cool if that's your thing. But I also notice you selling Kool-Aid and sugar from the kitchen. Isn't that called stealing? Man, you are the best Bible-reading thief I've ever met." He walked away laughing.

I went to my bunk, got out my Bible and read 1 John 1:9: "If we confess our sins, he is faithful and just to forgive us our sins, and to cleanse us from all unrighteousness." I confessed about the Kool-Aid and a lot of other stuff that day. Two weeks later the same guy asked me to bring some steaks back to the dorm. "I'll pay you two packs of cigarettes apiece."

"No," I told him, "I quit stealing—and smoking, too."

I read my Bible, prayed, watched my mouth and read the books the chaplain gave me. I found out the more I learned about Jesus the more I wanted to tell someone about Him. One day the cook I worked for started talking about all his women and how he loved them all. I kept my mouth shut. I knew if I opened it, I'd start talking about Jesus, and I was afraid I would do it wrong. Sure enough, I finally blurted out, "Do you know Jesus?"

"What?"

"Do you know Jesus?" I asked again.

"No, and if you say that once more I'm going to hit you in the mouth."

"Go ahead. You talked about what you love. Now I'm going to talk about what I love, and that's Jesus."

He ran out of that kitchen as though it were on fire. Next day I discovered he'd had another helper assigned to him. A few weeks later I met him in the yard. "Say, man, I know I freaked you out a while back. I'm sorry. You see, I'm a new Christian and don't know how to tell people about God. You were the first person I ever talked to except my dad and the chaplain."

"What happened? How come you wanted to be a Christian?"

"Man, all my life I've been blaming other people for my problems. I blamed God, white folks, my parents, everyone I knew. Except myself. I felt empty inside. And things just got worse and I couldn't sleep at night."

"Me neither."

"So finally one night I was by myself here in the yard."

"Here at Sierra?"

"Right here where we're standing. And it was like God said, 'Hey, man, when are you going to take responsibility for your own life?'"

"God really said that? I mean, is God real?"

"Listen, all I know is I have this kind of smile inside that I never had before and which I don't understand how it got there."

"Hey, can I become a Christian?"

"Sure."

"When?"

"I guess now. Just tell God it's your own fault you messed up, and ask Him to help you change." He prayed and as he did he cried. I didn't know what to do so I cried with him.

Then there was this older inmate named Zodiac. He really enjoyed giving me a hard time. One day a big crowd

of inmates was milling around the yard and as usual
Zodiac was needling me: "God is a myth. What kind of
God would let people starve? How come people get sick?"
Everyone was watching. I wanted to kick his butt.

"Maybe God exists and maybe He doesn't," I wanted to
say, "but I ain't taking your crap anymore."

"Come on, Sammy," someone called out, "you can't let
Zodiac get away with that."

"Stand up to him, Sam. Give him some proof."

"Yeah, give me some proof," Zodiac echoed. "If I could
see a miracle with my own eyes I'd believe."

"Okay, Zodiac," I responded. "You want to see a
miracle?"

"Yeah, I sure do."

I was plenty mad by now. "You get on your knees right
here, right now," I said, loud enough for everyone to hear.
"If my God, the God of heaven, doesn't touch your life
somehow, I'll denounce Him right here. But you've got
to get on your knees and say, 'God, if You are real, do
something for me now.'"

Boy, did it get quiet. Zodiac looked around in surprise.
"Man," he finally said, "I don't get on my knees for no
one."

I was starting to feel bold. "Well, Zodiac, either get on
your knees and call out to God to disprove me and the

Bible, or shut up and leave me alone."

Silence again. Men started to back slowly away as if they expected lightning to strike or something.

I stepped closer to Zodiac and said in a lower voice, "Man, it doesn't matter to me what you believe, but don't try to score off Christians because you think we're sissies or something. We might be meek but we sho' ain't weak, so cool it, man. Okay?"

"All right, brother Sam. I'll back off." We shook hands and parted.

I had a lot of bad attitudes of my own to work through. One night while I was reading my Bible in the empty mess hall, a guard walked up to me. "What are you reading?"

"The Bible."

"Do you believe what it says?"

"Sure I do."

"So do I." He looked at the page I was reading— Romans, chapter 13—and quoted the whole passage to me, line for line. I sat there with my mouth wide open. I didn't know God saved cops! I thought, *God must be getting hard up for friends if He's accepting cops.*

Pretty soon I found out, though, that He accepts all kinds of folks. The institutional baker and a long-time inmate started a weekly Bible study about this time. I was amazed at how many of the guys were Christians and I

never knew it. Up to this point I had had only the books
the chaplain gave me. Now I had people to talk to and
pray with. Different teachers came in from outside to lead
the Bible studies. This one guy named Bob Woodford was
a graduate of Berkeley. He used a lot of big words that no
one understood.

One evening I heard that some of the brothers weren't
coming because Bob was leading the study that night.
They felt that since they couldn't understand what he
said, why bother? I told them if they came, I would say
something to Bob.

As he started his lesson I stood up. "Bob, most of the
guys here have a sixth-grade education. When you use
big words to explain Scripture, man, we don't know what
you're talking about. Couldn't you use some words we
understand?"

Bob pulled down his glasses and looked at me over
them. "Is that where you people want to stay?" he
asked—and proceeded to teach exactly as he had before.

The nerve of that sucker, I thought. *Can you believe his
arrogance! He doesn't give a damn about us. I ought to
split his lip.* I didn't, though; I'd told the brothers I was
struggling to control my temper, and I knew they were
watching to see if I'd explode. Instead I took out a pencil
and paper. Each time Bob used a word I didn't understand
I wrote it down. He wasn't running me off. I'd show him:
That week I looked every word up in a dictionary. Soon I
began to appreciate Bob and his way of making us reach
beyond ourselves.

There was a guy in my dorm I noticed never had a
visit or even a letter. Jerome had been a drug addict for
many years; if he ever had a family they must have given
up on him. I told him about the M-2 program that Jess
had talked about, and Jerome signed up to get visits. I
didn't know that many of the visitors from outside were
Christians, but at least the man who came to see Jerome
was, because after a few visits Jerome told me he had
become a Christian, too. Soon Jerome became my closest
friend at Sierra.

Time was approaching for me to go before the release
board again, this time here at Sierra. I had been in prison
now 30 months. I asked Jerome to pray for me. "I just
want God's will to be done," I told him, but both of us
knew how badly I wanted to go home. I wasn't sure I
could take another year. One day I had seen a guy playing
his guitar out in the yard suddenly begin beating his
instrument against the asphalt. He had snapped. I heard
this could happen when someone was locked up too
long. The guards came to take him away but not before
making him pick up every broken piece. The guy cried as
he picked them up. I felt sorry for him. I wondered if this
could happen to me if I got another denial.

A few of us who were Christians had started gathering
nightly in the yard to pray. We made a small circle and
held hands, blacks, whites, Hispanics, Orientals, all
coming together as Christians. The rest of the inmates
made fun of us, but we kept meeting anyway. These guys,
too, promised to pray for my board meeting. Daddy said
he would be fasting.

Finally the day came. "Huddleston, B-36718, that's

Huddleston, B-36718. Report to classification for your board hearing."

I entered the room knees knocking. Sole power over my future was in these people's hands. Again there were two men present. One of them looked up from the stack of papers in front of them. "Huddleston, we've got some good reports about you here but the bottom line is, you haven't served enough time yet for the crime you committed. Any questions?"

"No, sir."

The other guy spoke up. "I suppose you thought this God trip was going to get you a quick parole."

I walked out thinking. *I want to go home. I want to go home. I was 17 when I was locked up. Now I'm 20 and I've got to spend another Christmas, another New Year's, another birthday, another Thanksgiving. Prayer doesn't change anything. I quit. I'm through with this Christianity bit! To hell with it.*

In the prison yard Jerome raced up to me. "What happened, Sam?"

"I got shot down another year."

"Sorry, brother."

"Sorry didn't do it; God did."

"Hey, don't blame God. Remember the thief on the cross?" Jerome had been going to the Bible study only a few weeks but already he knew more Scripture than many people brought up in church. "Jesus said, 'I will remember you.' But the thief still had to pay his debt to society. So do you."

"Damn society. Damn God. Damn everyone. Damn you. I quit."

"You can't quit! What about the rest of us?"

"Watch me. I'm not serving God anymore."

"Are you sure you ever were? Or did you just expect Him to serve you?"

"No, man. I really meant business."

"If you really meant business, Sam, you've got to stick to your guns."

I put my hands on Jerome's shoulders and cried. I didn't care who saw. I needed to cry, and I did. That board was the most devastating group of men I knew. They could drain all a person's hope in a matter of minutes, and almost seemed to take delight in doing it.

"I won't quit, Jerome. Sink or swim, I'm going all the way."

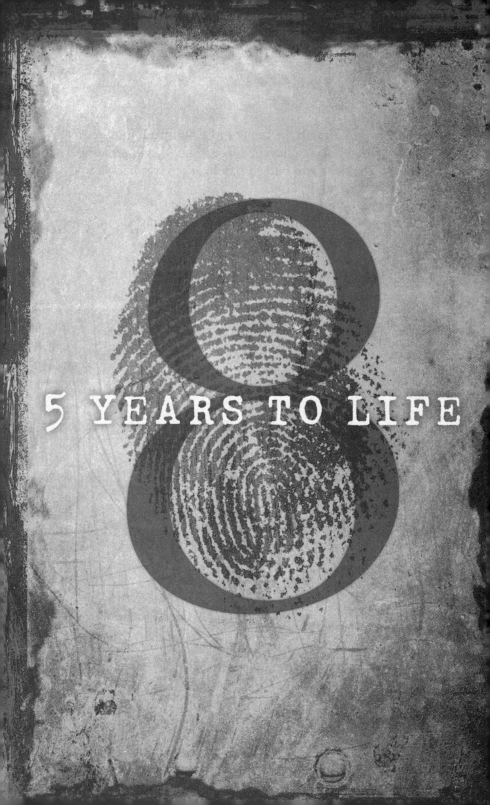

5 YEARS TO LIFE

WHEN THE STORMS OF LIFE ARE RAGING DON'T GIVE UP WHEN THINGS SEEM TO BE DISADVANTAGEOUS DON'T GIVE UP

Sierra was the headquarters for the inmate-staffed forest fire-prevention system serving all of California. Before being shipped to the various firefighting camps around the state we were put through a rigorous training program to make sure we were in good physical condition and understood the techniques and tools of the job.

My first assignment was to Mountain Home Conservation Camp located at the base of the Sequoia National Forest east of Porterville. Towering trees gave off fresh smells of pine and small piles of snow dotted the slopes. I could see for miles across a valley and almost forget the handcuffs I had worn on the way here. No towers, no fences.

The camp consisted of 80 men housed in cinder-box dorms. The routine was up by 7:00, clean your bed area, breakfast at 8:00, board your assigned bus at 9:00 and leave for the forest. We planted trees and cut underbrush, cleared firebreaks and built water towers. Back in camp by 4:00, dinner at 5:00, after which you could stay up as late as you wanted—which wasn't long after a day working out of doors.

That first night I stalled a while, building up the courage to do what I felt I had to do: kneel beside my bunk to pray. I knew that whether I knelt or lay on my back made no difference to God, but it was necessary for me. I had to signal the fact that I was a Christian, here where there probably weren't any others—which would mean I would have to live up to it. Convicts have a way of making you demonstrate your beliefs.

I sat on the side of my bunk, face in my hands, praying silently. Finally, when I had gained enough nerve, I spread my blanket on the cold cement floor and knelt on it. Behind me I heard footsteps stopping. Then more footsteps came up and stopped and still more. I could hear guys giggling.

The only words I could pray were, "Lord, don't let anyone kick my butt. If someone kicks me, Lord, I'll pull his leg out of its socket. Protect me, Lord. I don't want to let You down, but if I'm kicked, it's all over."

"What's wrong with him?" one of the guys asked.

"He's asleep."

"Naw, man, he's praying."

"He's what?"

"Praying. Maybe he's scared."

"Could be sick."

"Why don't we ask him?"

I prayed harder, "Lord, keep them away from me."

"Hey, man," another voice said, "let's leave the dude alone."

"Yeah," another echoed, "let's go outside." The footsteps retreated. Camp life was looser than at D.V.I. or Sierra. There were drugs and store-bought booze guys had their girlfriends bring up on visits. I was offered both but I always refused. One guy said, "'Ah, come on, Sam, God can't give you a high every day."

"The days He doesn't," I said, "He makes up for on the days He does."

One of the inmates, a guy named Phil, was involved in the M-2 program, the same one Jess and Jerome belonged to. Phil had his volunteer call me out when he came to visit, since my family hadn't been to Mountain Home yet. I ate roast beef and salad and enjoyed a lot of laughter.

I found out Phil's visitor was a Christian and that he was doing this out of obedience to Matthew 25:36. He quoted it to me: "I was in prison, and you visited me." I still found it hard to believe that anyone would come to a prison unless he was sent by a judge.

The guy seemed to really care about Phil. He became involved in both our lives. This was weird to me. I wasn't used to strangers caring as these M-2 folks did. I mean, the guy had to drive five hours one way each time he came. And he came up monthly.

He was the only Christian I saw, outside my own family, the nine months I was at Mountain Home. At Sierra I had had Jerome and the other Christian brothers and our nightly prayer meetings. Here at camp, out of 80 men, I was the only believer.

One of the guys on my crew, Gil, enjoyed riding me. "Hey, Sam, I've got a nickname for you."

"Good, you can keep it." I knew by his grin it was something degrading.

"Don't you want to know what it is?"

By this time the rest of the crew was listening.

"No, thanks."

"Well, I'll tell you anyway. It's Reverend Jones."

This was a local pastor who had been in the news for embezzlement from his church. I stopped working and looked at him.

"What's wrong, Brother Sam, the truth about the faithful hurt?"

I didn't answer him. I was too angry. "Jive sucker," I said under my breath. "If he calls me Reverend Jones again, I'll call him Pillsbury Chocolate Doughboy. He's short, round and dark. I'll see how he likes that."

"Hey, Reverend Jones!" The other guys picked it up.

I opened my mouth to respond with "Pillsbury Chocolate Doughboy," but nothing came out. I tried again, and again no words came. Maybe God was helping me change, after all.

One morning I glanced out the window and stared in disbelief. It was snowing. I had never been in a place where it snowed. In a few days Daddy and the rest of the family would be up to visit me. I hoped they would bring Andre. He was 3 years old, and I wanted him to see the snow.

Sunday morning they called my name over the intercom. I ran through the snow to the visiting room. There they were—Daddy, Doll, Cynthia, Rhona, Murphy . . . and Andre. Buddy and Tony were both in the Army. I kissed Doll and my sisters, hugged Daddy, shook Murphy's hand and scooped Andre up in my arms.

"Do you know what that white stuff is?" I asked him.

"Grandpa said it's snow."

All of us went outside and had a first-rate snowball fight. I noticed, though, that instead of throwing them, Andre kept trying to put the snowball in his pocket.

"What are you doing, son?"

"I'm taking it home to show Mommy."

May came. Fire season.

We filed off the bus one morning for the first of many days of battling blinding heat and smoke. The foreman pointed at the mountain. "Put on your gear, men. We will be climbing that mountain, cutting a firebreak so if the fire reaches that point, it will stop."

Smoke was rising high and in the distance we could see low, smoldering embers from burning brush. The dark gray clouds overhead indicated it had been burning for a while. The number of firefighters present suggested it would be a while before it was out.

I was a little scared. So far we had never fought a fire. I put on my backpack, which had my food and other necessities, filled my canteen with water, checked the flashlight on my helmet and sat on the sandy ground with the others until we were called. I found myself praying and, with the little sunlight that was left, reading my little New Testament.

"All right, fellas. Line up. It's time to show these guys what we can do."

I wasn't sure we could do too much. I was happy to learn, however, how great they fed you when your shift was up.

Days when there were no fires to battle, I worked in the chow hut. My job was to keep the tables, walls and floors clean, and refill salt and pepper shakers and napkin holders. The only thing I hated about the assignment was waiting on the lieutenant. He wouldn't get his own food as the other guards did; he wanted to be served. I had to ask him what he wanted as he walked through the food

line, then fix a plate for him and bring it to him after he
sat down.

One day after lunch, I grabbed my Bible and sat under a
tree reading the Gospel of John. I came to chapter thirteen
and read how Jesus washed the disciples' feet. That really
blew my mind. Jesus was the Son of God. Why was He
washing feet? I didn't get it. But if Jesus could wash the
feet of His disciples, then I could serve the lieutenant.

After that, every day as I set his plate down, I whispered,
"Jesus, for You." It really made a difference.

A Christian radio station broadcast out of Bakersfield.
I listened to it while I was cleaning up the kitchen. It was
another thing that helped me. I finally wrote and thanked
them. They wrote back. I wrote again, sending them a
poem I had written. Three days later I was astonished to
hear them read it on the air. I sent a few more and they
read those, too. I was beginning to feel as though I really
had it together.

Then one night Gil—who had come up with the
nickname "Reverend Jones"—and I got into an argument.
I opened my big mouth and called him every foul name
in the book, the whole dorm hearing it. Gil split to the
recreation room to shoot pool. I was left thinking, *How
come I do so well, then all of a sudden I explode?*

I sat on my bunk and tried very hard to concentrate on
the Bible. No good. I knew I had to apologize and I didn't
want to. I tried praying about it. *God, help me.* It was
beginning to dawn on me that His taking control of my
life involved more than I thought.

I got up and walked slowly to the pool room, trying all the way to figure out another way to apologize without saying I was sorry. Gil was shooting pool with another dude. I turned to leave. Saying I was sorry to him was one thing, but in front of someone else was another matter. As I reached the door I remembered I had no trouble belittling him in front of others.

"Say, man," I mumbled.

"Yeah, Reverend Jones?"

"Uh, could I, uh, say something?"

Gil stopped shooting pool and looked at me.

"I, uh, just wanted to, uh, say that I was sorry for the way I talked to you just now. Would you forgive me?"

Gil put down his pool stick and stared at me. To my horror I discovered I was crying. What a weakling! Then I could see that under his shades Gil was crying, too. *What a sick trip,* I thought, *two convicts crying in the poolroom because one of them asked for forgiveness.*

"You know," he said at last, "this is my second time in prison. The first time I did four years, and now I'm doing four more."

"That's a lot of time."

"Yeah. I've been in Chino, Soledad, D.V.I., Tehachapi and San Quentin. I've seen a lot of guys turn religious. But you're the first one who has made me want to be a

Christian. I know you hate it when I call you 'Reverend Jones.'"

"Then why do you do it?"

"I don't know. Just being ornery I guess. Anyway, I want you to know I think you're a for-real brother."

That was the greatest compliment any convict could pay another. "Thanks, Gil. You are, too."

"I'll try to be, Rev—ah, Sam."

In February I was returned to Sierra for my third release board appearance. I sat in the waiting room thinking, *What if it's another year's denial?* The thought made me sick. I wanted to go home. I was tired of jailhouse lies and power games, tired of lives going nowhere. I sat there thinking of Mr. Bill, a guy in his 50s I met at Mountain Home.

"Sam," he had told me, "I've watched you since you got jail-house religion. Stay with it when you get out, son. I've been screwing the state for 20 years, only I've supplied my own butt. I've destroyed my life getting even with people I thought were to blame. I've blamed everybody—my parents, friends, ex-wives. Now I know I'm the only one who could change things—and it's too late."

"Mr. Bill, it's not too late."

"For me it is."

Now I heard, "Huddleston, B-36718, go on in."

My throat was dry, every nerve on edge. Entering this room was always scary. The two board members sat at the table—different men from last year.

"Huddleston?"

"Yes, sir."

"How much time have you done, 42 months? And you're in here for second-degree murder-robbery, is that correct?"

"Yes, sir, it is."

"Tell me, what are your plans if you are released?"

"To find a job, sir, and preach the gospel."

"You've written here you want to follow the footsteps of your father. Is he a preacher?"

"No, sir. He is a deacon."

"So you want to spread the good news, huh?"

"Yes, sir."

"And you'll go wherever you feel the calling and wherever the money is."

"Sir?"

"Oh, I know your type, Huddleston. You're in prison, so you get religion and try to fool everyone into thinking you're a reformed character. You were involved in killing a man! You and your partner killed another human being, and you're not even sorry. Get out of here. You'll get your results in the mail."

They didn't have to mail them. I knew the results: another year. My feet refused to function. I knew better than these guys what I had done. I also knew how sorry I was for it. But they wouldn't believe me.

"Huddleston, I said get out of here. And take your phony God with you."

"Yes, sir." I headed for the door. As I grabbed the doorknob, I turned around and said, "Sir, you may not believe me, but I am sorry for what I did. I also understand why it's hard for you to believe that Jesus Christ has changed my life. But one day I'll be released, and then you'll know. How? Because I'm never coming back!"

The following fire season my crew was sent to California Men's Colony West at San Luis Obispo. I couldn't believe there were so many old guys in this camp. Some were on crutches, others in wheelchairs, some had artificial limbs. This was blowing me away. My crew leader told me, "Sam, these guys will die in prison. They started out young thinking they could whip the system. They were given two years here, three years there, nothing major. They always figured, man, this ain't no biggy, I can do the time. Now, 30, 40, 50 years later the system is all they know. They get out, break windows, steal something, just enough to violate their parole and get back in prison. They don't know anyone outside. They've lost touch with their families. It's over for them—they've lived the majority of their lives in places like this. Look at their faces . . . they tell the whole story."

That night I couldn't sleep. I couldn't get the faces of those old men out of my mind, especially this one old black guy. His large flabby arms and sagging chest let me know he had once lifted weights. As I had stared at him his face had changed into mine. *Oh, God,* I prayed, *please don't let this be my end. With Your help, I ain't never coming back to prison again! Never again will I give anyone this much power over my life. I'm taking control, with Your help.*

At the end of the fire season, I was returned to Sierra. Daddy had been telling everyone about the change in me, and one day I got an invitation to speak at the church in Livingston that I attended as a boy. To my surprise, the prison authorities granted permission. I was sweating the entire hour ride and didn't talk much to my guard escort. In Livingston we drove down Third Street. I pointed out all the lawns to the driver that my brothers and I used to mow.

We arrived at the church an hour early. Only the pastor was there to meet us. "Hello, Sammy. We're sure glad they let you come. We don't know how many will be here but we're expecting a crowd."

The guard let me walk around, entering the classrooms, remembering when Daddy was Sunday school superintendent here. When time for the service drew near we went into the sanctuary. I sat on the front row unable to look behind me.

In a little while the pastor motioned me to join him on the platform. I walked up, sat down and for the first time saw the church was packed, with people standing in back and along the sides. Daddy was about halfway back, his face split in this huge smile. I had brought my Scofield Bible along; I remembered when Daddy said he'd save it for me because someday I'd be preaching from it.

I opened it to the story of the Prodigal Son and talked about how Daddy didn't give up on me and God never did either. Then in the back I saw a familiar face. George. George was the one who ratted on Shep and me—told the cops he'd seen us go into the liquor store. I kept speaking but my anger was rising. The nerve of him showing up! George and I had partied together, gotten drunk, smoked dope together—and he snitched me off.

When I finished my talk it seemed like everyone in the place wanted to shake my hand and tell me they were praying for me. Some of the old ladies even hugged me.

As I shook hands with the last person, I noticed George waiting in the back. "Hey, Sammy, I really enjoyed your speech."

I couldn't answer. Here was my "friend" who had ratted. The guard looked puzzled when I didn't take the hand George reached out to me. I wanted to tag him on the jaw. I wanted to hurt him bad. I wanted him to feel how it felt to be locked up.

George started to back away. "Sammy, I came to say I'm sorry I told on you. I didn't think they'd send you away."

"It wasn't your fault. Had me and my cousin not gone to the store, you'd have had nothing to tell." I couldn't believe I said that.

"Then you forgive me, Sammy?"

"Of course I do."

Shaking his hand, all the bad feelings I had harbored against him for four years seemed to drain away. I let them go. This, too, was a part of my life I was taking control of—or letting God take control of—getting even. I vowed that day to drop all grudges I was holding against folks. If I didn't, it was a sure ticket back to prison.

Six more months dragged by. Daddy wrote that he was working at finding me a job for when I got out. Many of the guys I saw coming back to serve second and third terms reported that they hadn't been able to find work. No one wanted to hire an ex-felon. So they returned to the only thing they knew—selling drugs, robbing folks, stealing and forging checks.

In February 1976, 12 months after the previous hearing, I appeared before the board again. I was nervous, but not like before. I had learned a lot about life from those denials. It goes on. When I thought I couldn't take another day in this place, I did. Through it all I was learning to have a deeper trust in God. The Bible studies and Scripture memorizing really helped. I went to my board appearance quoting 1 Peter 5:7: "Casting all your care upon him; for he careth for you."

"Huddleston, B-36718, you're next."

I entered the room. There, behind that long mahogany table, sat two different men. Never in all my board appearances had I seen the same men twice.

"Huddleston," one of the men asked, "do you have a job?"

"Not yet, sir."

"If you get a date, can you get a job?"

"Yes, sir."

"It appears you have done extremely well these past few years."

"I've tried, sir. I hope you won't take this wrong, but I hate this place."

"I just hope that when you get out you'll continue hating it. Most don't, you know. Eight out of 10 come back."

"Remember," the other guy spoke up, "on parole you're still in prison. There just aren't any walls. We can pick you up anytime and bring you back. You have any last remarks?"

"No, sir. May I leave now?"

"Yes, unless Mr. Pitts has something he would like to say."

"I would like to say something. Huddleston, you're

a lucky man. I've been on this board long enough to remember guys the same age you were when you were arrested dying in the gas chamber at San Quentin for the same crime. You're a lucky man."

"Yes, sir, I know. I'm blessed."

"Blessed, lucky, whatever. I just hope for your sake that you never come back. Remember your sentence—five to life. Next time we'll keep you till you die. You'll get your results in the mail."

I almost ran out of there. I wanted to believe I got a date, but I didn't want to be let down. I continued to pray—not to get out, but for whatever it took for me never to return to prison. Even if it meant another year here. I realized I would rather do another year and learn my lessons than get out and be sent back.

The next day it was hard to work. All I thought about was the results from the board. When the mail was delivered, I was handed a piece of paper folded in half and stapled. On the outside it said, "Adult Authority Board." I looked up to see the others watching me. I pried out the staple, peeled back the paper slowly and read: "HUDDLESTON, B-36718. THE ADULT AUTHORITY HAS GRANTED YOU RELEASE ON PAROLE EFFECTIVE SEPTEMBER 6, 1976."

Even though I had the paper in my hand, I couldn't believe it was true. *I'm going home. I'm really going home. I'm leaving this hell . . . alive.* I yelled, "I got a date! I got a date!" I grabbed my towel, went to the shower and cried, cried and cried. I had made it through this place.

When I phoned Daddy with the news, he had some good news for me, too. The owner of the plant where my brother Murphy used to work said he would hire me. He wrote a letter to my counselor verifying the job. I was given credit for the 90 days in county jail after my arrest and 60 days off for having a job. That made a five-month time cut and moved my release date up to April.

The night before I was going home, I couldn't sleep. What if I got back in trouble? Would I leave God at the gate like so many? Would I make good on my job?

The next morning I was ready to go at six o'clock. But departure time wasn't until nine. I had brushed my teeth four times, taken two showers and combed my hair until my scalp was sore.

When breakfast came I grabbed a tray and went through the line knowing it was my last meal there. As the bowl of oatmeal was ladled out I realized I had actually grown to like it. But this morning I was too excited to eat much.

"Say, man," I said to the guy who sat down next to me, "you want some more oatmeal?"

"Hell, no, I can't eat that crap."

"Yeah? How much time you got?"

"Two years."

I grinned. "You'll be eating it before you leave this place." At 8:50 I was standing at the back gate. A few of the Christian brothers who didn't have work duty showed

up. I hugged them, some for the last time this side of
heaven; others I would see outside. Jerome had a date for
the coming fall; his M-2 friends were helping him relocate.
"God bless you guys." I walked away and didn't look
back. Somehow I had to wipe that place out of my mind.

I was dressed in the clothes Daddy had sent for me to
wear home. I got into a van and was driven to the front of
the prison. There stood Daddy and Murphy, all smiles.

On April 9, 1976, after four years, nine months and one
day, I walked through the gates a free man. We got into
Daddy's Volkswagen. Before he even started the engine he
prayed, "Lord, Sam is free. Some folks don't think he'll
make it but You and he are going to make liars out of
them. Thank You, Lord, for giving me back my son."

Daddy drove me to Modesto where I met my parole
officer, Mr. Hughes. When he had finished laying out the
rules I looked at him and said, "Mr. Hughes, you don't
have to worry about me. I'm not going back."

"Yeah, yeah, yeah. I've heard all that before."

"I know you have, but not from me. You have no idea,"
I told him, "what that place has done to me."

The trouble was, I didn't know either.

REMEMBER YOU ARE TRAVELING DOWN A ROAD THAT HAS AN END BE CAREFUL AS YOU TRAVEL TO HAVE A FAITHFUL FRIEND

From Modesto we drove to Daddy's house. As I walked down the short sidewalk I thought, *I left this house 10 years ago, searching for answers, and everything I ever wanted was right here.*

From a drawer in the kitchen Daddy drew out a sheet of lined school paper—the note I had written when I ran away from home. From another drawer came a book of matches. Together Daddy and I watched that letter blacken, curl and turn to ashes.

All of the past, however, was not that easy to dispose of. Sunday I went with Daddy to the church in Merced where he had been made a deacon. It was much larger than the church in Livingston where we had gone as children and most of the faces were strange to me. Right away I was put on the spot by Pastor Amey. "Brother Sam, we've been praying for you for quite a while. Is

there anything you'd like to say?" I wanted to run out
the door.

I stood up and said, "Thank you for praying for me
while I was in prison," and sat down. I had the same
feeling I had had when I went to those A.A. meetings in
D.V.I. "Hi, I'm Sam, I'm an ex-con."

After church I walked around the old park in Merced.
I couldn't believe my eyes when I saw the same old guys
still hanging out selling the same dope in the same place. I
had been gone from the streets five years and nothing had
changed. I knew I wouldn't be hanging out here. I didn't
want this to be my future.

Monday morning I was at work at 7:30 A.M. Daddy
drove me since I hadn't gotten my driver's license back yet.
They issued me a hammer, nail bag and measuring tape. I
couldn't believe I would be making $3.50 an hour. I had
made 90 cents a day at the camps, $10.50 per month at
D.V.I. The plant manufactured prefabricated roof frames
for homes. I found out one of the guys working there was
a Christian. We worked in different parts of the plant,
but at break time Rick and I got together. His pastor,
Reverend Smallwood, lived right across the highway from
the plant and Rick invited me to eat lunch over there
with him. We met at noon at his car and drove across the
freeway.

Rick entered the house without even knocking. "Norma,
it's me, Rick! Come see who I brought for lunch."

A lady came down the stairs smiling at us both.

"This is Sammy Huddleston. Sammy, this is Norma, Reverend Smallwood's wife."

I had brought lunch with me, but Mrs. Smallwood gave me some soup to go with it.

I sat there wondering if she would treat me the same if she knew I had just been released from prison.

That afternoon at work I noticed this guy wearing a T-shirt that said "Property of Alcatraz Prison." I walked over to him and asked if he was trying to be funny.

"What are you talking about?"

"That T-shirt. You trying to say something?"

He looked at me real weird.

"Listen, I don't know what your trip is. I bought this shirt months ago up in San Francisco."

"Then you don't know about me?"

"No, and from the way you act, I don't want to know you."

"Hey, man, I'm sorry. It's just, I thought, well, anyway, catch you later."

Somehow I had assumed that the entire plant knew I was an ex-convict. I felt it was written across my back or something.

After work, Daddy took me to the Department of
Motor Vehicles so I could reapply for a driver's license
and drive Buddy's car. He had left it home when he joined
the Army. I passed the road test and the written test with
no problem, but almost strangled over a casual question
by the inspector. "So where have you been for five years
without a driver's license?" he said, just being friendly.
"Prison" is a short word, but it was hard to get it out.

Now that I had wheels I could get up to Oakland and
visit Andre who was almost 6 years old. Ann had moved
up there a couple of years earlier. When I got my first
paycheck she let me take him shopping and buy him some
clothes.

Every day Rick and I went over to eat lunch at the
Smallwoods'. One day Reverend Smallwood came home
at noon. He told me he and his wife had known about
my prison record all along. "Sammy, would you consider
speaking at our church, sharing your testimony?"

That's how, the following Wednesday, I was sitting on
the platform at the Smallwoods' church. When I stood up
to speak, though, words wouldn't come. I stammered and
stuttered and finally said, "Let's pray." As I was praying, I
looked up and saw a lady in the fourth pew whose house
I once had vandalized. I had never been caught, never
confessed to it. I had the feeling I needed to. I decided I
would, right after service. I concluded my prayer and tried
again to speak, but once more could only stutter. I looked
straight at the lady and called out her name. Everyone
called her "Big Mama."

"Six years ago, Big Mama, do you remember when

someone cut up the clothes on your clothesline and broke up some furniture in your home?"

"Sure. I remember."

"Well, I'm the one who did it. I'm asking you now to forgive me."

"Sammy, I knew it was you, and I forgave you a long time ago."

I spoke that night better than I ever thought I could. I couldn't figure it out, but I think it had something to do with asking Big Mama to forgive me.

I wondered if the bad stuff I had done was the reason for the knot I felt at times in my gut. I couldn't pray it away. Maybe instead of praying for it to go away, I needed to ask God to show me what caused it. The more I did this, the more I recalled the people I had hurt. Everywhere I went memories taunted me. Memories of mugging someone, fights, stealing something. I knew God had forgiven me but was something else needed?

Atwater was the place to start. I drove down B Street and stopped in front of a blue-painted house. I walked up to the door and rang the bell.

"Sammy Huddleston! Come in. What brings you by?"

"Mrs. Wright, when I was a teenager, I showed a lot of disrespect toward you by the way I treated your daughter. I've come to ask you to forgive me."

She stood there with her mouth open.

"What did you say?"

"I'm asking you to forgive me for how I acted around your daughter, and for showing disrespect to you and Mr. Wright."

"I can't believe what I've just heard. No one has ever asked me to forgive them for not respecting me. I do forgive you, Sammy, and I'm sure Jennie has, long ago."

As I drove away, Mrs. Wright was standing on the porch waving.

I visited so many people, asking forgiveness, that I lost count. I found it hard to believe I had hurt so many people. At age 16 I had gotten into a gambling debt; Mother Carrie loaned me $200 to cover it, which I had never repaid.

I got a money order for $250 and gave it to her with this note:

> Dear Mother Carrie,
>
> Six years ago you loaned me this money. It's time I paid you back with interest. Thanks for being such a great granny.
>
> Sammy

The process of seeking forgiveness was an exhausting one—emotionally, physically and spiritually. 'Most everyone forgave me after getting over the initial shock. A few could not, nor could I ask forgiveness of the man I had injured most, the store owner whose death I had brought about. Some debts were too enormous ever to repay.

One Sunday I asked Pastor Amey if I could help out with the youth program. I knew as an ex-con I needed to keep busy doing right things. We put on regular events for the teenagers at church, and went on outings with other groups.

Pastor Amey's pretty young sister, Linda, was one of the youth workers. I found out she was divorced with two little kids—Royce, age six, a few months older than Andre, and Ericka, age four. I liked talking to Linda. We talked about the young people, her job at the phone company, her family and my family. I never met anyone who made me feel so good by just listening. She didn't try to answer all my questions. The more we were together, the more I realized I had never talked to anyone that freely without having to watch my back later.

One evening as I drove her home after a youth meeting, I ran a red light. I started to shake and couldn't stop. I pulled over and sat behind the wheel trembling.

"Sam, what's the matter?"

"I don't know, Linda. I had this flash that I was arrested."

"For running a red light, Sam?"

She had no idea the terror I had of going back to prison. I kept hearing the man on the parole board: "You're still in prison; there just aren't any walls."

One day at the plant I got a visit from my old buddy Wayne.

"Hey, man, I hear you got, you know, religion. I hear you don't party anymore."

"Wayne, when I was in prison no one from the old crowd came to visit me. Not one person in five years. Who did come, whenever I needed Him, was Jesus. No one knows what hell those five years were. I promised myself if I could stand up for God in prison, I could do it out here. I don't drink anymore, I don't take drugs, and I quit smoking cigarettes when I became a Christian."

"I hear ya, man."

We talked a little more and he left. I knew we weren't buddies anymore. My parole officer came by twice a month. I had to urinate into a bottle so he could test it to see if I was using drugs. I hated how humiliated I felt coming out of the bathroom at home holding that little bottle.

As I entered a store one day to buy a soda, it dawned on me for the first time that I wasn't 17 anymore. I could buy my own beer. I stood in front of the beer case staring at the cold cans. I wondered if it still tasted the same. I mean, what was a beer? One beer was not going to get me drunk or anything—even if it did violate parole. I reached for the glass door and stopped, terrified. I was the only one in the place who seemed to hear it—a hideous clanging noise. It was the cell at D.V.I. being opened. I turned and walked quickly from the store with beads of sweat on my forehead. I had made it this time.

Linda and I kept seeing each other. She was a real lady. She wouldn't get in or out of the car unless I opened the door.

"Linda," I told her once, "you're my best friend. Whenever I'm with you I feel good inside."

Linda smiled. She had wavy brown hair, a coffee-and-cream complexion and the most beautiful smile in the world.

We took the young people to a weekend camp. We hadn't been at the place 20 minutes when Linda sprained her ankle playing volleyball. By evening it had swollen to twice its size. I made her a cane from a tree limb but, for the most part, I carried her from place to place the entire weekend. I knew before the weekend was over I wanted Linda to be my wife.

I drove some of the teenagers home, then Linda. I carried her into her house and got a pan of warm water for her ankle. I knelt down in front of her and massaged her foot. After a few moments, I looked into her eyes. "Linda, do you think you could ever—I know it's an enormous thing to ask—but could you possibly ever be willing to share your life with an ex-convict? What I mean is—will you marry me?"

"I wouldn't marry an ex-convict, Sam. But I'll marry you.

Why do those five years in prison define who you are? The man I know is strong and kind—and free of the past."

It was the most wonderful thing anyone had ever said to me. If only I could be free of the past! If Linda saw me that way, maybe there was a chance.

On August 21, 1976, Linda Gail Amey became Linda Gail Huddleston. We were married at the church where my grandfather's funeral had been held. Her brother performed the ceremony. The church was packed with relatives and friends.

Now I was married, with a family, and scared. I didn't know how to be a good husband or father, so I read books, any book I could get my hands on that I thought would help me.

Royce had a hard time trusting me. After all, he had been the man of the house for quite a few years. Ericka, on the other hand, started calling me Daddy immediately. But Linda's aunt had been against the marriage because of my record. When Ericka went there to spend the night, she started crying.

"What's wrong, Ericka?" her aunt asked.

"I want to go home. I want my daddy to come get me."

At 11:00 that night the phone rang at our house. Though it was 30 miles away, I went to get my daughter. The aunt later told Linda I must be all right if Ericka responded to me as she did.

I spent time praying and playing with the kids and doing the things my daddy had done with us. We went swimming in the canal, had picnics and visits to the zoo. Royce and I went to some local football games together. I would sit up late at night and look at pictures of them when they were babies. I stared at these pictures for hours, imagining that I had known them then.

I also talked about their father with them. When we had family prayer I made sure we prayed for him. "Ericka and Royce," I told them, "I'll be glad when I meet big Royce."

"Why?"

"So I can thank him."

"For what?"

"For my being a part of your lives. Do you know if he and your mom hadn't married, you'd have never been born and I'd not have the honor of raising you up?"

Andre came to visit after the wedding. I'll never forget his and Royce's first meeting. Royce was almost 7; Andre had just turned 6.

"Royce, this is Andre. Andre, this is Royce," is all I said. They ran outside to play, but soon came running back into the house, out of breath and wide-eyed.

"Daddy!" demanded Andre, pointing a finger at Royce. "This guy says you're his dad!"

"Tell him whose dad you really are," insisted Royce. I smiled. "I'm both your dads."

They digested this in silence.

"You mean we're brothers?" said Royce.

"That's right."

They looked at each other and went back outside arm in arm. I figured I'd have plenty of time to explain the details later.

"Sam," Linda would ask me often, "what is it that you want to do with your life?" I didn't know, except I knew I wanted to serve God in some way.

"Then shouldn't you think about going to school? If God has a call on your life, then you should start thinking about getting prepared."

"School? I don't want to go to school." I was married, with kids. It was too late to think about education.

Still, at work, I shared the idea with Rick.

"Man, Sammy, that sounds great. Have you thought about Bethany Bible College [now Bethany University]? The Smallwoods' two sons go there."

"Is that a fact? Maybe I'll talk to them about it at lunch today."

Both Norma and Robert thought Bethany was a great

school. They had gone there themselves.

"Sammy, I think Linda is correct," Reverend Smallwood said. "After all, what do you plan to do when you've given your testimony everywhere? People won't come to hear a testimony over and over, but they will return to hear God's Word preached."

That evening I prayed, "Oh, God, You know I want to please You. If You want me to go to college, then please make a way. Lord, I don't have a lot of confidence in myself. Only You know what those years in prison did to my self-esteem. If this happens, it will be You who does it."

I called Bethany and asked for an application. The following week I filled out the forms and mailed them in. I was especially worried about the money. I filled out a Basic Equal Opportunity Grant Form; under "Employment previous year," I wrote, "Prison." Internal pressure was mounting: I had been out of prison eight months, gotten married, had a family, a parole officer, bills to pay, and now college.

Linda and I waited and prayed. She even put in for a transfer to the phone company's office in Santa Cruz. That really scared me. What if she got transferred and I wasn't accepted? But Linda kept saying, "We're God's responsibility. We belong to Him." I was accepted at Bethany and Linda's transfer came through as well.

People from the Wednesday night Bible study we attended came over to help us pack. They also gave us some money they had collected to help us with the move. I was learning a lot about Christian friends. My old friends and I only took. These folks gave.

"Sam," one of the brothers said as he helped me load the U-Haul, "we know it's been tough on you, and it will probably get tougher, but hang in there. We'll be praying."

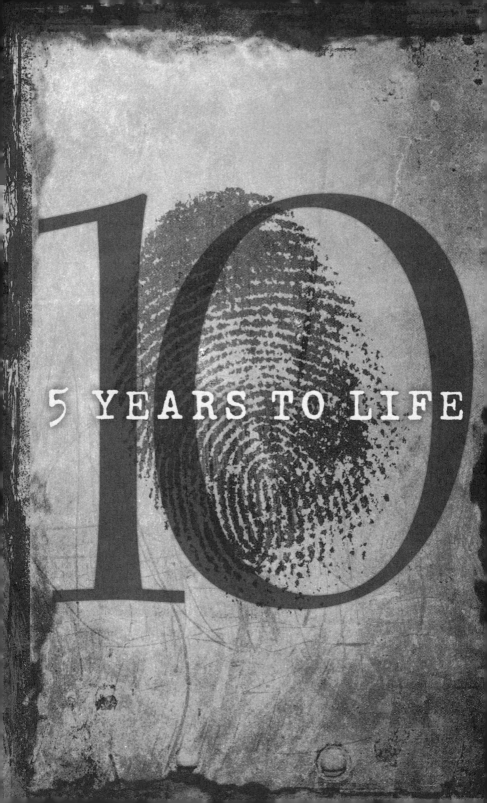

5 YEARS TO LIFE

LIFE IS NOT A GAME
YOU SIMPLY WIN OR LOSE
LIFE IS A MAP LAID OUT
TO FOLLOW IF YOU CHOOSE

Linda and I talked all the way to Santa Cruz. My gift to our marriage was one of worry. Linda's was one of faith. She reminded me how the government grant had come through, and how we were headed to a duplex in Santa Cruz where housing was "impossible" to find. She had taken a "disconnect" call from a customer there, and on a hunch had asked if they were leaving a rental. They were, and had been worried because there was time left on the lease.

Our duplex was located on top of a hill at the end of a cul-de-sac. As I parked the U-Haul, Royce jumped out, grabbed his skateboard and stepped up onto it. I will never forget how large his eyes got as his board picked up speed without his pushing it. He was used to the flat ground of Merced.

We unloaded the truck and set up our beds so we wouldn't have to sleep on the floor. When bedtime came, however, I couldn't sleep. I put my clothes back on and drove the two miles to the Bethany campus. The winding gravel road led through huge redwood trees. I parked and went into the unlocked chapel. I sat down and looked up at the high-beamed ceiling barely visible in the light of a single bulb. My only thoughts were me, B-36718, going to college. In my wildest dreams this was never a part of it.

Oh Lord, I'm scared. Never in my life have I had responsibility. Now I have a wife and children who are counting on me. Please help me to make it in school and as a father and husband. Don't let me fail.

In class that first day, I glanced nervously at the other students. I wondered what they would have thought if they had known I was an ex-con.

"Be seated, please," said the professor. "I'm going to pass out the syllabus." *The sylla—what?* I said to myself.

"Let's go over it together. Number one: The course title is Pentateuch. There will be four mini-papers and a 15 page term paper at the end of the course."

Term paper, mini-papers? What's he talking about?

"All papers must be typed."

Typed? I can't type. I don't even have a typewriter. How am I going to make it? I may as well drop out right now.

We were instructed to come Wednesday prepared to take notes. Notes. The only notes I had ever taken were those given to me from girls in high school.

My other three classes were the same format: lectures, mini-papers and term papers. I went home panicked. I had to read 200 pages by Wednesday. Two hundred pages! I walked through the door of our duplex and went straight to bed. My head was hurting and I was ready to quit.

I woke up barely in time to pick up Royce at school and Ericka from her day-care program.

"What's the matter, Dad?" Royce asked. "Oh, nothing, son."

"Then how come you look so sad?"

"Yeah, Daddy, you look awful sick," Ericka chimed in.

"It's school."

"You don't like it?"

"Naw, it's . . . it's just that I have to do a lot of things I've never done before."

"I know how you feel, Dad. I felt the same way today when I started second grade."

"Yeah, me, too, Daddy. I was scared at the nursery today." Royce looked at me. "I did what you told us to do."

"What was that, son?"

"I prayed. I prayed, and Jesus helped me."

"So did I, Daddy."

"Oh, Ericka, you're just copying me."

"No, I'm not, Royce. I really did pray."

Back home I headed again to the bedroom, this time
not to sleep but to ask forgiveness of God for doubting
His power. "But Lord, I'm so scared." Scared of the
classes, scared of failure. I had never completed anything
in my life. I dropped out of high school. I dropped out
of my family by running away and using drugs. What if I
couldn't stick out four years of college?

The kids and I picked up Linda at work. "How was
your first day?" she asked eagerly. "Was it exciting? Tell
me about each of your professors."

"Hold on a minute! First of all we have to take notes,
write term papers and read a lot of books. I don't know if
I can handle it."

She looked at me and smiled that lovely smile. "Don't
worry, hon. The Lord hasn't brought you all this way just
to see you fail."

I had a lot of problems with the reading assignments.
I didn't know how poorly I read. I sat at my table with
the book in one hand and a dictionary in the other.
Sometimes I wept with frustration. Here I was, 23 years
old and couldn't keep up with the 18-year-olds in class.
What helped was to come across one of the words Bob
Woodford had used in the prison Bible study, words I had
looked up afterward. Finding those words in a college
textbook was like meeting an old friend in a strange city.
I kept hearing Bob's voice: "Is that where you want to
stay?"

In class I started sitting in the front row. I recalled when I was in high school all the goof-offs sat in the back. For the first time in my life I *wanted* to learn. I had to. I listened closely as the teacher lectured and wrote down everything I thought was important. When I got home, I rewrote the notes.

I also studied my classmates. They all seemed to look the same—blue eyes, blond hair and rosy cheeks. They had no resemblance to the scowling, scar-faced convicts I had lived with for five years. Their language was a lot different as well. I felt as though I stood out like a sore thumb. I couldn't help but wonder again what the kid next to me would think if he knew what I really was.

When the time came for the first exam, I hadn't studied. I didn't know how, and I had too much pride to ask anyone for help. The professor passed out the test. I filled in my name, guessed at the true-false questions, then walked up to the desk and handed it in.

"Through already, Sam?"

"I didn't study."

"Come by my office later this afternoon," he said.

When I knocked on his door he jumped up and took some books off a chair. "Sit down, Sam. How's it going?"

"Lousy."

"Why's that?"

"Because I'm 23 years old and I don't even know how to study for a test. Boy, what a dunce!" Then I told him about my life, and going to prison and receiving Christ.

"Sam, you've been out of school for what, six years, five of them in prison?"

"Correct."

"Most of our students here are just coming out of high school. They're in the habit of studying. You haven't studied in six years, and before that I dare say you didn't hit the books too hard."

"You're right there, man." Most of the time in high school I had been so stoned I couldn't tell you what the question was, let alone the answer.

"Now listen! You can do it, and you will do it. But it's going to be a long, slow process. Don't try to compete with these kids. You can't. Set your own pace and keep with it. Where are your notes?"

I showed him and he gave me a few points on taking notes and studying. I left that meeting on cloud nine. Here was a smart, educated man who believed in me. Before long, though, the truth of what he said about the process being slow plunged me to the depths again. After failing my third straight exam I came home one day and told Linda, "I quit."

"You what?"

"I said, 'I quit.' What makes a man a minister, anyway?

Education? No way! I don't need an education to be a preacher. God can use anybody and anything. He just needs a willing vessel, right?"

"I remember, Sam, reading in the Old Testament about a jackass God used to speak to a prophet."

"So?"

"So that shows you're right: God can use anything. But I also remember reading in the New Testament where God used Paul, and he was a very learned man who had studied under the best teachers of his day."

"Uh-huh, so?"

"So you have a choice. You can either be a jackass or you can be a Paul. And whichever you choose, I'll still love you and stand beside you."

I didn't want to hear that. I wanted to quit. I wanted to quit before I failed. But after what she said, I knew I couldn't. I went back to school more determined than ever not to become a jackass.

I saw a lawyer and he helped me adopt Royce and Ericka legally and give them my last name. We joined a local church. I knew that one essential for the Christian life was belonging to a local body. Though I was willing to give my testimony, the pastor never asked. He told me once, "Sam, many pastors would love to have you in their church to use you."

"How do you mean?" I asked.

"They'd have you up front, speaking, teaching a class, doing jail ministry. But my concern is your growth as a child of God."

I didn't really understand, but I felt that he cared about me. So I brought my family to Sunday school, attended a class, and afterward we all sat together during the service. It was great.

In the church bulletin one Sunday I read about an upcoming fishing camp for fathers and sons at a place called Hume Lake. Royce was nearly 7 now and had never been to a fishing camp, so we went. We really bonded on that trip; I kept thinking how my stepfather and I could always communicate out in a boat.

As I worked on building a relationship with the children, I began to notice how edgy I was around Linda. I wanted to know exactly where she was when not at work. When I didn't know, I would blow up.

"Sam," she said one day, "you don't trust me."

"What do you mean, I don't trust you?"

"You know exactly what I mean. Don't play games."

"Well, if you must know, you're a woman."

"What's that got to do with anything?"

"My mama was a woman and she left me. I promised myself no woman would ever hurt me like that again."

"Sam, I'm not your mother. And I've never given you a reason to mistrust me."

"That's right, but you're still a woman."

There were other problems we faced at this time. It seemed in spite of the grant and Linda's job, we could never make ends meet. I started working after school. Then I got a second job, alternate nights, and then still another part-time job. I was working three jobs and we still didn't have enough. I had little time to study, which made me increasingly frustrated. As I sat one day going over a pile of bills, Royce came up and asked if he could go play with his friends. "No!" I yelled. "That's all you do, play. You never clean your room, you don't study and you're always asking me for money." Royce started to cry. He got Ericka who had seen the whole thing and they went to their bedroom. I could hear them both crying.

When we picked Linda up from work, they told her how I had yelled at Royce.

"What's wrong, Sam?"

"Nothing," I barked.

"See, Mom, there he goes again."

"Shut up, Royce," I said.

Ericka started crying again.

"Quit crying!" I shouted at her.

"Sam, you don't have to yell at the kids. If you've got a problem, we can talk it out."

"I don't want to talk. I don't want to deal with this. I want out." The pressure valve had gone off. "I'm an ex-con. You don't seem to understand that I can't make it. I can't make it in college and I can't make it as a father. The pressure is too much and I want out."

Silence.

In prison I couldn't vent my frustration for fear of being written up by the guards and given more time. Earlier I never learned to handle anger either. Someone made me mad, I'd fight. But now here I was, and still unable to control my temper. When we got home, I went into the house and punched the refrigerator. "Oh, God, I need help."

But things only escalated. The jobs were tearing me apart so I quit all three. Then I sat around and worried about how we would pay the bills. I couldn't talk to Linda without yelling. So I didn't talk to her. If I had something to say, I wrote her a letter, and she wrote me back. I was failing in school and at home.

I went out driving late one night and bought some beer. Running was all I knew and I was doing it again. I had to, I told myself. I couldn't handle the pressure . . . two kids, a wife, bills, college, freedom. I wasn't Superman.

I drove around until the beer was gone, then went home. I went to bed on the sofa so as not to wake Linda. I was afraid if she found out she would leave. If my probation officer found out about the drinking, I would be on my way back to prison.

I started taking long walks. When I returned from one of them I asked, "Linda, could I talk to you in the bedroom?"

"Sure, Sam."

"Linda, can you ever forgive me for flying off the handle the way I do? I know I've been blowing it. I can't make any promises but I'm going to try to do better."

She smiled as if she knew something I didn't. "Sam, I love you. Nothing can change that. Sure, you blow it at times, but so do I. God's hand is on your life, Sam. Yes, you're an ex-felon—but how long are you going to use that as an excuse? You will always be an ex-felon, but you can choose not to be a failure."

The door opened slowly. I looked up and saw Royce and Ericka peeping in.

"Come here, kids."

They both jumped into my arms.

"Daddy, I love you," Royce said.

"So do I," Ericka echoed.

Linda and I embraced. This is what I wanted, a happy family, but I had no idea how to make it happen.

Then a guy I had known in prison came to visit. I found out that he, too, was filled with anger and having a hard time adjusting to society. The key, he said, is learning to handle that stuff before it handles you. "You need some counseling, man, or you won't make it. I did 10 years and I've got so much junk inside me it ain't funny. Man, I yell at my old lady for serving cold food."

"I do, too." I would tell Linda, if it's supposed to be hot, then serve it hot. I had had enough cold food in prison to last me a lifetime.

"Sam, I bet you explode a lot, too, don't you?"

"Man, you have no idea how often I explode. I pray a lot but it doesn't seem to help."

"Listen, you've got to get the poison that's in you out. The only way I know how to do that is talk to someone. Do it before you destroy your marriage and end up back in prison."

The person I found to talk to was the last man on earth I would have expected—a real super-smart professor. I had gotten mad at him in class because I asked him a question and was told to go to another student for the answer.

Later that day I stormed into his office. "Do you know who I am?"

"Apparently not."

"Do you know where I just came from?"

"No. Should I?"

"Listen, I'm a parolee. I've got a life sentence hanging over my head for robbery and murder."

I was trying to impress him with how tough I was, but he just smiled and asked me to take a seat.

"Now, let's start from the beginning. My name is Norman Arneson. You may call me Norm if you'd like. What's your name?"

"B—I mean, Sam."

"What's the problem, Sam?"

I didn't know why, but I started spilling my guts to this guy. I told him of my struggles at school and at home. I told him I had failed at everything I had started, and was afraid I wouldn't make it this time either. I talked about prison—the humiliations, the never-ending fear.

It was the first of many talks. He became a friend, counselor and mentor. He also taught me a lot about prayer. One night when I was visiting in his home, he suggested we pray. There was some classical music playing in the background. As he prayed, I couldn't get over the fact that he didn't turn the music off. Another time, as we analyzed a Bible passage, I asked if we could pray. His response was that we already had. Talking, he said, was a form of prayer. Wow! This was different. I wondered what the brothers in Sierra would think of this. We used to use special language when we prayed, a special tone of voice. And here was this college professor who acted as if prayer was an everyday thing.

Linda and I invited him over for dinner one night. I told the kids that one of my college professors was coming over for dinner. Royce was so nervous at meeting him—as he put it, "a real-live professor"—that as he shook Norm's hand, he called him "Professional Arneson."

With "professional" help I completed two semesters with C's and B's and not a single D. When summer came, I got a job at a lumberyard. It was out of doors and I really liked the change from sitting in a classroom. Ann let Andre come visit for an entire month. Royce, Andre and I went fishing and rode skateboards and had a lot of fun. I also spent many nights talking to Andre about his mother and me. I didn't want him growing up filled with anger the way I had. Many nights I sat in the kids' room talking not only about Jesus, but also about our family and how God brought us all together. We'd pray for Ann and Big Royce, saying, "Lord, maybe we can't be a family down here, but You can help us be one in heaven." I hated the day Royce and I drove Andre home. We made arrangements for him to come visit every month.

During one of our talks, Norm suggested I give my testimony to his class. He thought it would help me overcome my fear of rejection from the other students.

I entered the classroom the following Monday like a man going to the gallows. "Class," Norm said, "one of your classmates has a testimony he would like to share. I've asked him to do this, so please give him your attention."

For the next 10 minutes I told my story to the scrubbed and shining faces before me. Then I sat down and waited for the heavens to fall. Instead, one by one, the students came over to shake my hand and tell me how proud they were that I was at Bethany. Some even hugged me. My only remaining fear, that I would be asked to leave the school once their parents learned of my background, never materialized.

The spring of my junior year, Linda started school, too. She quit her job with the phone company, and though I got a job with a maintenance company I didn't make nearly enough to support my family. Linda and I started preaching and singing at different churches on the weekends and the offerings we received helped out.

The semester ended with my starting my ministerial internship program at Craig Memorial Chapel on campus. Professor Arneson was the pastor and the membership comprised not only many of the students and instructors but people from the surrounding community as well. The internship lasted the entire summer. I worked at the church in the morning and for the city of Santa Cruz on a county-funded program for kids in the afternoon.

At the close of summer I began my senior year. I had to take 16 units in order to graduate with my class in May. One of the classes was *Hermeneutics*, the art and science of studying Scripture. I knew it would be a tough one, requiring 20 small papers, five or six typed pages each. After finishing six semesters, I figured I knew the ropes, and so I procrastinated on getting started. A month before the due date, I started working like a madman, spending up to five hours in the library each day. By putting all my concentration on it I made the deadline, but fell behind in my other classes.

My stomach started bothering me, too. I didn't pay it much mind until it got to the point where I couldn't sleep because of the pain. I finally finished all my courses, but my stomach continued to hurt.

Linda kept after me to go to the doctor, and I kept reminding her we didn't have the money. Eventually, however, I had to go. The doctor diagnosed an ulcer. "Obviously, young man, something is eating away at you. This prescription will help, but it won't cure you. You need to deal with the real problem, whatever it is."

The medication made the pain subside temporarily, but then it returned and worsened.

About this time Mama arrived for a visit. I had been working for a couple of years on writing my story down, but so far Mama had refused to read it. One evening while she was at our house I brought the manuscript into the living room. "I want you to listen. I'm going to read you something."

I read her a few sentences. Then I handed her the manuscript. "Please read it, Mama."

"Okay, baby. I'll read it tonight."

I prayed before going to bed, "God, please use what I have written to bridge the gap between me and my mother."

The next morning I leaped from bed and ran into the kitchen. Mama was up drinking coffee.

"How did you like it, Mama?"

"I liked it; it's good. Only it has some errors." My heart sank; I just knew she was going to chew me out for some of the things I had said.

She turned to where I had written, "Mama walked out and never came back."

"Mike, that's not true."

"It isn't?"

"I did come back."

"You did?"

"I came back four or five times, trying to work things out with Edward. I took all of you to Los Angeles with me, but Rhona got sick and I took you home. Finally I realized your father could make a better home for you, with Mama Carrie's help, than I could. The hardest thing I ever did was to say good-bye to my children."

I stood there holding back the tears. I was 26 years old and all my life I had hated my mother. Even since being a Christian, I had found it hard to love her. I had always thought she just left us. I had blamed her for my rebellion. I hadn't known she cared about us. I hadn't known. All those years of anger and hurting other people . . . feelings of rejection . . . I just hadn't known.

I told her I'd be right back. I went to my bedroom and cried. I was so happy to find out my mother really loved me! I realized I had always feared I must have done something as a child to make her leave.

I went back to the kitchen, and she showed me other places where I had it wrong. I changed the manuscript to match the facts. When I finished all the changes, I noticed that the pain in my stomach was gone.

Later I wrote a letter to my mother:

Dear Mom:

I wanted to sit down and write you a letter expressing to you how I feel. There had always been two things I needed to know. One was, did you love me as a child, and second, do you love me now? After spending these past few days with you, I can truly say I know you've always loved me. I'm not writing this because I'm afraid to tell you. I want you to have my feelings in writing so when those times come that you feel that no one loves you, you can get this letter out and reread it. For the first time in my life, I can truly say I love you, Mama. I really do. Thanks for being my mother.

Graduation day arrived. Two guards from Sierra came, and also the chaplain who had the discussion group there. So many friends and all my brothers and sisters.

As the graduates marched into the auditorium I looked over to where my family was sitting. Linda—no one knew better than I how much her love and belief in me had to

do with my being in this procession. Royce, Ericka and
Andre were jumping up and down in their seats. Mama
and Dad were there. Not only had God brought me and
Mama together, but my stepfather had joined a church
and stopped drinking. I knew John and I would be going
fishing again soon. And, of course, in the center of them
all—Daddy, his entire face one big grin.

"Samuel Michael Huddleston."

As I approached the podium to receive my degree, I
almost thought I could see Daddy Bryce sitting there, too.
I could almost hear him say, "You've made me proud of
you, grandson, very proud."

EPILOGUE

May 6, 2006. Family and friends have traveled from across the country to join the graduating class at Regent University in Virginia Beach, Virginia. Seated in the audience, and at the center of my attention, is my wife of 30 years. Near Linda are our three children, their spouses, our eight grandbabies, my parents, and my oldest brother, Buddy, representing my siblings.

I've completed my doctoral program. My dissertation, "Multi-Ethnic Leadership Development in the Northern California/Nevada District of the Assemblies of God" is an outgrowth of so many ministry opportunities God has given me.

I hear my name. "Samuel M. Huddleston."

I rise, walk across the platform, shake the hand of the university president, and receive my D.Min. degree. It has taken me five years.

And in this moment of elation, I feel a wash of dread flood my spirit.

There was another program that took five years of my life. Another place where my name was called and I would rise and obediently follow the man in front of me.

For an instant, the light seems to dim and I sense those old prison walls.

Then I feel God's peace restored.

This is the new you I had planned all along, His Spirit whispers.

I look into the audience. My parents are crying. But their tears are tears of joy. There is no trace of the sorrow that gripped them as they ran from a courtroom long ago, a judge's sentence ringing in their ears.

"Samuel Michael Huddleston, I sentence you to . . . state prison . . . for no less than five years and no longer than the rest of your life." Luck could not preserve me during those years. It took providence. That providence grips me and propels me toward a future as bright as every promise of God.

It has been an amazing 25-year journey since I graduated from Bethany College (now Bethany University) in 1981.

I suppose the roots of my doctoral dissertation go back to my years as a child in Livingston. I was 10 years old, watching my father's black and white TV in the living room. There on the news I saw policemen with German shepherd dogs and firemen with fire hoses separating a peaceful civil rights march of teenagers in Birmingham, Alabama. I said to myself, *If I ever have the chance to show the world that blacks and whites could do something together, I'd do it.* It took years before that opportunity presented itself at Church on the

Hill in Vallejo, California, where I began ministering as an associate pastor after leaving Bethany. Pastor Terry Inman and his staff enriched my life immeasurably. They also helped me come to grips with some of the remaining darkness I battled.

At Church on the Hill I had to confront my own prejudice. You couldn't make me believe that as a black man I was prejudiced. I often told my friends, "You can't be prejudiced when you're the 'prejudee.'" But ministering in Vallejo's rich cultural mix and watching Pastor Terry make the greatest use of everyone's gifts, I gained new insights into how all-encompassing is the body of Christ.

Serving among Church on the Hill's youth, I discovered my need to continue in ministry preparation. A girl came to my office and told me her father had molested her. I didn't know what to tell her. Once I got beyond, "Let's pray," I hardly knew what to say.

That motivated me to earn a master's degree in marriage, family, and child counseling at Azusa Pacific University. Those counseling classes pried into my soul and uncovered emotional baggage I had continued to haul around—my unforgiveness and my anger, basically toward my mom.

My mother and I began to build a relationship. Today, I'm the one of her six children responsible for her finances and estate. Her trust means the world to me. The restoration of love between us has been a balm in our lives.

Andre was also restored to me. He eventually came to live with Linda and me permanently. The day Andre and I fully reconciled was another of heaven's gifts.

We had taken a group of young people to a YWAM (Youth With a Mission) conference in Hawaii. One of the sessions was on unforgiveness, and Andre and I took a walk on the beach when it was over.

"Will you forgive me, Dad?" he suddenly asked.

"For what?" I said in surprise. I'd been looking at the palm trees and the ocean. I hadn't noticed he was crying. His voice trembled, as he looked me in the eyes.

"For hating your guts."

"Why do you hate my guts?" I asked.

"You never were there. You got my mom pregnant. Then you were gone." He continued with a litany of things I could tell he had rehearsed.

I forgave him. Then I asked him to forgive me.

Andre eventually graduated from Bethany. He's now married and has two children. He named his firstborn after me . . . Samantha.

Royce and I have remained close. Royce is someone who calls it like it is.

"Dad," he once asked years ago, "you've written a book, you've met President Reagan, you do television and all this stuff. How come you don't let this go to your head?"

For a moment, God's blessings flashed before my mind. I felt a rush of elation. It quickly faded.

"Do you know what your daddy was in prison for?" I asked.

"Yeah," Royce said, "you and some other guys robbed this guy and he was killed."

"Son, until he comes back to life there's nothing in this world that will make your daddy get a big head. You have no idea what I live with."

Royce is married with two daughters and a son. He is involved in the youth ministry that he loves so much.

And of course there's Ericka. She has blossomed into Linda's beauty. She has a wonderful husband and three beautiful daughters. She is still the apple of her daddy's eye.

Graduation day at Regent brings all of them together. My love for each of them wants to burst out. And yet, in that moment of joy, I remember the tears I have wept so many times because of the pain I've brought to so many people.

"Samuel," the Holy Spirit keeps whispering, "this is where I've wanted to bring you all along. There are so many lives I want you to touch."

I understand the grace of God. I really do. Because I need it every day. Some people don't feel like they need that grace every day. I know better. God's grace reminds me there are no prison walls stronger than His divine freedom.

I served with Match-Two Prison Outreach, which for years was the largest one-to-one prisoner visitation program in the nation. For six years I served as president.

One day as I was touring a prison with the warden I found myself back at my old cell. I was trying to communicate with the guys in there and tell them I had been in that cell. But there was so much noise in the cellblock they couldn't understand me.

And it was like God said to me, "That's right, I took you out of this place. Now I want to get this place out of you, so you can really live."

I've tried to communicate that hope to other prisoners, and I believe God has used me to connect in ways other ministers really can't.

I was speaking at a banquet at San Quentin. An older guy, walking with a limp and using a cane, came up to me. He looked at Linda and said, "You know, I was in prison with your husband years ago." She hugged him. She always makes those guys feel special.

"Was he a good boy?" she asked.

"He was a good kid," he said with a smirk. But he knew good and well I wasn't a good kid. Then he looked at me and said, "You know, youngster, when I get out this time I'm going to make it."

"Why is that?" I asked.

"Because listening to you tonight gave me hope."

I started to weep.

Linda would often tell me this is what my life gave to prisoners, but it was not until this moment that I understood.

Match-Two was an opportunity for God to send me back to the deepest recesses of my life. I'd allowed the poison from the past to paralyze me in the present. As a result of going back to those prisons for six years, I finally became free.

That freedom grew in other ways. At a 1990 family reunion I was asked to speak to several hundred close and distant relatives.

"The Prodigal Son came to his senses after he destroyed the family name," I said. "After he had spent the family money."

I looked at my great-uncle (now deceased). I'm his namesake. "Uncle Samuel," I said, "I'm the only one of your nieces or nephews named after you (he had no children) and I shamed you. I shamed your name. Would you forgive me?" He began to cry.

I looked at cousins, aunts and uncles. "I have no idea what it felt like to walk the path you had to walk because of my actions. I ask you to forgive me."

My dad was there. "All I can do is ask you to forgive me," I said.

I just stood there with my head down, sobbing. For years I had not gone to family reunions. I was just too embarrassed and ashamed.

My older cousin, Major White, the one who had asked me to come and share what it was like to meet President Reagan, was the first to speak. "Samuel," he said, "we forgive you."

It was a Jacob experience. I went from Jacob to Israel with my family.

Eventually, I returned to Atwater, the community scarred by my crime. I forced myself to go, and I decided I would return to that store. When I went back, the store had been torn down. It was a parking lot. I sensed the Spirit of the Lord saying to me, *That's what I've been trying to tell you. It's buried.*

I went to a breakfast where I had been asked to speak. I stood before the business leaders of the community. The county sheriff, the chief of police and other dignitaries were there. I was nervous and scared.

"Some of you are too young to remember," I said. "Others of you are too old ever to forget the shame and the hurt I brought to this community. I just want to begin by asking you to forgive me."

There was silence. Then one after another head across the room began to nod in agreement. A wave of forgiveness flowed through that room, a room not 200 yards from a parking lot where every trace of my crime was now erased, except in the lives of those I hurt.

My stepfather died in November 2003. The graveyard where he is buried is also the resting place for the victim of that fateful robbery. I stood at that grave. "I'm sorry," I said. My stepfather's loss was the connection that gave me that opportunity.

And now, May 2006.

I hear my name. "Samuel M. Huddleston."

I grasp the hand of Regent's president.

But I feel a different hand in mine. It's scarred, like my soul. And it's gently leading me on.

ENDORSEMENTS

"As my wife and I were reading this book, tears began to course down our cheeks, as we recognized God's grace in this man's life. Sam Huddleston is not just a friend; he is someone I admire as a man of commitment, conviction, and character. I recommend this book for those who desire a deeper understanding of God's grace."

Donnie Moore
Radical Reality

"*Five Years to Life* is the true story of how a prisoner fell in love with Jesus and turned his life upside down. This book has helped many who sit behind prison bars, but it speaks to all who desire to know the freedom found in a Christ-centered life."

Senator Tim Leslie

"Dr. Huddleston graduated from Bethany College, now University, in 1980, as one of the many milestones of his remarkable journey. Sam's life serves as an example of courage, faith, and determination, and the perpetual love of both his earthly father and his Heavenly Father. *Five Years to Life* is a must read for anyone who has ever felt like giving up. I highly recommend it."

Maximo Rossi, Jr., Ph.D.
President, Bethany University

"Don't buy this book—unless you are looking for a hard hitting, fast-paced, can't-put-down book that reads like a ride in a getaway car!"

Ben Kinchelow

"Sam has captured the essence of the Father's love which is perseverance and compassion and hope. This book should be in the hands of every man and woman behind bars and in the hands of every man and woman who ministers to them."

Ed Peecher
Founder, Bishop, Chicago Embassy Church

"As a mother who's had the painful experience of visiting a son in jail, my heart was gripped by Samuel Huddleston's story. It also gave me hope. Hope that it's never too late for one right choice to change a lifetime of wrong ones. In *Five Years to Life*, Sam tells how he chose Jesus and it made all the difference. What a privilege it is now for my husband, Jim, and me to be "serving time" with Sam and Linda in ministry, seeing them make a difference in the lives of others. 'If the Son sets you free, you will be free indeed' (John 8:36)."

Judi Braddy
Author of *Prodigal in the Parsonage, Simple Seasons* and *It All Comes Out in the Wash*

"As a police officer for 34 years, I can say the young Sam Huddleston was a typical drug/alcohol-addicted street punk. He was in prison because that is where he belonged. So what happened? How could Sam Huddleston now work hand in hand with police officers as a police chaplain? How could he become a respected member of our community? *Five Years to Life* answers these questions by telling a real life story of a man's struggle to change. We can all learn from Sam's struggles and celebrate the man he is today. *Five Years to Life* is a must read for any of us seeking changes in our lives."

James E. Trimble
Chief of Police, Benicia Police Department

"From the skirmishes on the streets and in the prison to a life
of service to mankind is what the gospel of Jesus Christ is all
about. Sam is a 'living espistle.' "

Glen D. Cole, D.D.
Pastor Emeritus, Capital Christian Center, Superintendent
Emeritus, Northern California-Nevada District of the
Assemblies of God

"From my years of jail ministry, I know this book will be read
by inmates in both jails and prisons. For many it is—at least
in part—their story. Inmates will not want to put it down. It is
simply enough written for those with limited education. What
inmates need is hope and that's what this book delivers."

Pat Argue

"Prepare for a great blessing as you read how God had a plan for
Sam Huddleston's life and how Sam was raised up by God from
a prison cell to be a leader in the Christian community. I consider
it a great privilege to serve the Lord with Sam and I know *Five
Years to Life* will bless the hearts of those who read it."

Harry L. Greene
President, Good News Jail and Prison Ministry

"God's permanent, loving redemptive transformation in Dr.
Sam Huddleston's life through the glorious redemptive work of
Jesus Christ on the cross, His blood, and His resurrection, gives
anyone eternal hope that God is indeed a forgiving God who is
not a respecter of persons. Sam is truly a new creation in Jesus
Christ and a shining star as he proclaims and lives out, with
much joy, credibility and conviction, the righteousness of Christ
through the message that changed him, the gospel, as you will
see for yourself in his captivating story *Five Years to Life*. Sam,
my friend, is a faithful warrior for God and a passionate lover
and defender of people, who clearly demonstrates his gratitude
to God for His amazing, constant grace in his relationship with

Jesus Christ and others. Sam is an amazing communicator and engaging master storyteller that points people to where the real action is at: the Cross and Christ. Sam has a magnetic, contagious, humorous, friendly and joyful personality that hooks people immediately, like it did me 16 years ago. Sam is the real deal; I know! Sam's credibility is the permanent fruit of the people he serves and loves, which is rooted in his marriage and relationship to his wife, Linda, in whom Sam delights as he validates his love for God."

Manny Mill
Executive Director, Koinonia House ® National Ministries

"*Five Years to Life* is an inspiring story about God's amazing and transforming love. It is one of those rare books that, once you begin reading, cannot be put down. Readers of all ages will be inspired and encouraged by Sam's story of brokenness and restoration."

Randy Fiorini
Farmer, Turlock, California

"As the Warden of the Deuel Vocational Institution where Dr. Huddleston was locked up many years ago in his youth, I highly recommend his autobiography, *Five Years to Life*. His story is not just about paying his debt to society as an inmate, but more a story of lessons learned, personal responsibility, growth and leadership, family love and spirituality. For those incarcerated, his book gives a *blueprint* to freedom and all will be inspired."

Claude E. Finn
Warden, Deuel Vocational Institution

"In a time when life's circumstances and the consequences of one's choices can result in discouragement and despair, the life and story of Samuel Huddleston emerges as a lighthouse in the midst of a raging storm to serve as a rock of encouragement and hope. I wholeheartedly recommend *Five Years to Life* to all who could use a lifeline tossed their way."

Dave Buehring
Founder and Executive Director, Lionshare Leadership Group

"Dr. Samuel Huddleston's personal story is a true representation of hope in the midst of a dark world. *Five Years to Life* is a powerful story that grips your heart from the first to last page. As I continued to read, it was hard for me personally to remember that I knew the main character within this book. Dr. Huddleston's life is one of both integrity and character. It is humbling to see firsthand the miraculous hand of God and transformation that has taken place in his life over the years. This book will be a blessing and encouragement to anyone no matter what season of life they are traveling through."

Abe Daniel
District Youth Director
Northern California-Nevada District Youth Ministries

"We are proud of how Sam has allowed God to use him for His glory. My wife, Sharon, and I met Sam when he was a prisoner at Jamestown. We were involved in prison ministry there with Chaplain Gene Anderson. We have continued to watch God bless and use him and know him to be a true servant of God. We know his book will be a blessing to all who read it."

John and Sharon Wright
Golden Altar Ministries

"Is there hope for one who has been in prison? Is there a future for one who has been involved in crime? This book, *Five Years to Life*, describes how Sam Huddleston experienced the power of God. He tells how God restored him from brokenness into a new person with possibilities in life. He is a testimony of what God's grace can do to a person. Furthermore, how God prepared him to be a leader who serves others."

Willie Tjiong, D.Min.
Director, Doctor of Ministry Program
Associate Professor, Regent University

"There are over 7,000 men in our facility and we have a large percentage of that number participating in the Protestant Chapel program in three separate locations within the prison. I have used this book extensively throughout the Correctional Training Facility (Soledad Prison) here in Soledad, California, for several years now. It continues to be one of the most popular books checked out by inmates in our chapel libraries, as it gives each and every reader a glimmer of hope. *Since God did it for Sam Huddleston he can do it for me!*

"Sam and Linda Huddleston have a genuine love for God and His people, which is evidenced in particular when they come to minister in one of the three services we conduct every Sunday behind these prison walls. Sam is very well received since he has been where they are, which prepares them to hear what the Spirit is saying to the church. Linda's ministry at the piano and in song is the catalyst that softens the hardened hearts to receive the nuggets of truth shared by this couple who are totally dedicated to doing the will of the Father.

"I highly recommend the book and their personal ministry."

Rev. Judge C. Lindsey
Protestant Chaplain, Department of Corrections and
Rehabilitation

"Samuel Huddleston—once lost, now found—exemplifies the courage it takes to make it on the inside and out. Whether your prison cell is surrounded by bars, a mind tormented by regret, or a life filled with discouragement, *Five Years to Life* creates hope. Reading through these pages will inspire you to see people, not as who they are, but as what they can become."

Char C. Blair
Founder and Executive Director, Unspoken Ministries
www.unspokenministries.com

"This book is a must-read. My comeback was in my career; Sam's comeback was in his life."

Dave Dravecky
Former Pitcher, San Francisco Giants

"This fascinating true story of God's marvelous working in the life of one rebellious young man can do nothing but challenge every reader with its amazing message."

Ted W. Engstrom, World Vision

"*Five Years to Life* is a compelling book; it has the kind of stimulating drama that only comes from real life."

Don Smarto
Director, Institute for Prison Ministries

"Once you start reading, you begin rooting for him to be an overcomer and he does! *Five Years to Life* is an inspirational story for anyone at any age because it proves that Christ can make a difference."

Reverend Mother Consuella York

"This story gives hope to the hopeless and help to the hurting—no matter who they are."

Chaplain Ray

To contact Sam Huddleston,
write him at:
P.O. Box 995
Benicia, CA 94510

Or visit his Web site: *www.samhuddleston.com*

Also available by Dr. Huddleston:
Grand Slam, a story about two men discussing
how to cover the bases of life

Onward Books, Inc.
4848 S. Landon Court
Springfield, MO 65810
417-425-4674

Visit our Web site: *www:onwardbooks.com*